THE
VOODOO DOLL
SPELLBOOK

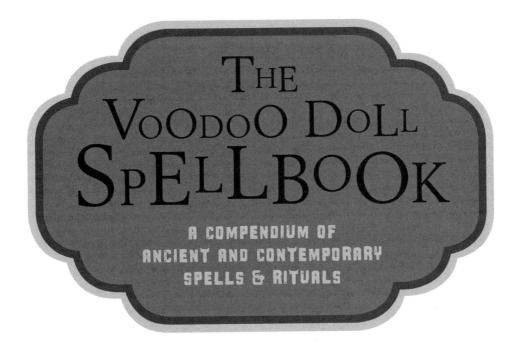

THE VOODOO DOLL SPELLBOOK

A COMPENDIUM OF ANCIENT AND CONTEMPORARY SPELLS & RITUALS

DENISE ALVARADO

WEISERBOOKS

San Francisco, CA / Newburyport, MA

This edition first published in 2014 by Weiser Books, an imprint of

Red Wheel/Weiser, LLC
With offices at:
665 Third Street, Suite 400
San Francisco, CA 94107
www.redwheelweiser.com

Copyright © 2010, 2014 by Denise Alvarado
Foreword © 2014 by Dorothy Morrison.

ISBN: 978-1-57863-554-2

Library of Congress Cataloging-in-Publication Data available upon request.

Cover design by Jim Warner
Cover photograph © Shutterstock / Fer Gregory
Interior by Deborah Dutton
Typeset in Adobe Caslon

Printed in the United States of America
EBM
10 9 8 7 6 5 4 3 2

CONTENTS

SEVENTEEN Spells for Self-Improvement   159

EIGHTEEN Wishing Spells   165

NINETEEN Japanese Voodoo Spells   171

Disclaimer and Legal Notice

The information contained in this book is strictly for educational purposes. If you apply ideas contained in this book, you are taking full responsibility for your actions. Magic, Voodoo, hoodoo, and energy work are faith-based systems, meaning if you do not believe in your own power to effect change, change is unlikely to occur. Since these factors differ according to each individual, there is no guarantee of your success or improvement level. The author and publisher assume no responsibility for any of your actions, whether you use the information for positive or negative purposes.

Much of the information contained in this book is drawn from folklore collections, recipes given to the author from family, friends, customers, medicine men and women, and healers over the span of a lifetime, recipes from 19th and 20th century formularies, historical accounts of African-based folk magic from slaves in the southern United States, objective evaluation of anthropological literature, and from the personal grimoires of the author. The information contained herein is subject to the interpretation of the author.

The information contained in these pages is not meant as a substitute for the advice of health or mental health professionals.

Readers should use discretion before performing any rituals or spells.

FOREWORD

The very utterance of the term "Voodoo doll" probably evokes more visions in the mind's eye than any other in the modern vocabulary. It doesn't matter whether you're a magical practitioner. It doesn't matter if you believe in magic. Regardless of your spiritual path or what you hold true, it still conjures up visions of dark, steamy bayous and oak trees dripping with Spanish moss, a weathered old Swamp Witch stabbing pins into an effigy, and a magic so powerful that nothing—not even the Gods—can alter its course.

But does that sort of magic really exist? And if so, is it still viable in today's modern world? More to the point, though, can someone really learn how to use it effectively?

It does. It is. And you can.

To start with, doll magic has a head start over other types. Why? Because the doll—in and of itself, regardless of shape or form—holds a magic all its own. It's a silent, timeless, irresistible force to which no one—not toddler, nor teen, nor even adult—is immune. It tugs at our emotions and urges us to care for the doll, dress it, and occasionally, even confide in it. And since that sort of emotional response is the driving force behind all magic, it's little wonder that Conjure Folk find the doll to be such an indispensable basis for their workings. They simply add the proper herbs, oils, symbols, charms, and personal items, couple those with firm intent and focus, and—voila!—wind up with a spell so potent, it will stop at nothing to hit its mark. It's quick and easy—and exactly the kind of magic geared to today's busy lifestyles.

That's all well and fine. But how do you know exactly which components to add? Or how to be sure you won't mess things up?

Not to worry. *The Voodoo Doll Spellbook* has you covered. Written in an easy-to-understand style, Denise Alvarado—an accomplished Conjure Woman and teacher of the magical arts—answers every question you could possibly ask, as well as a few that have probably never crossed your mind. She's jam-packed this book with spells and recipes to meet every need, along with complete step-by-step instructions. What's more, she's provided you with all the tools necessary to take charge of your life, change your circumstances, and finally become the person you were born to be.

So take the first step toward living that brand new life. Turn the page. And let the magic begin!

Dorothy Morrison
Author of Utterly Wicked
www.wickedwitchstudios.com

PREFACE

I can't guarantee the effects of **Voodoo** dolls. But if you believe in it, it will surely bring some changes to your life.

Yang Min

Since the beginning of time, people have created and used dolls in an effort to control the situations, places, people, and things that surround them. Growing up in New Orleans, I had the opportunity to hear many curious tales and beliefs related to the infamous Voodoo doll and I was privy to witnessing the same. Doll magick fascinated me then, and it fascinates me now.

In this book, *Voodoo doll* is used as a catch-all term to describe dolls used in magic and ritual throughout time and across cultures. Any old-time rootworker, however, will use the preferred terms *conjure dolls, doll babies, dollies*, and *baby dolls*. In anthropology, one will find the terms *fetich, fetish, poppet, puppet*, and *effigy*. Still, the term *Voodoo doll* has reached academia as a means of denoting a doll that is used for magickal purposes regardless of culture, and as an academic I am following suit.[1] Nonetheless, let me be clear that my use of the term *Voodoo doll* does not imply that all of the spells contained in this volume are doll spells from the New Orleans Voodoo and hoodoo traditions. There are spells from ancient Greece and Egypt, from Malay, Japan, Africa, the European grimoires, and plenty from hoodoo and New Orleans Voodoo. For each spell, I use the doll term that seems appropriate for that tradition and context.

The spells contained in this book are based on studies of doll magick and folklore across cultures. I have collected a large number of these spells for my personal enjoyment, and had planned on including all of them in this book. Once I began writing everything down, it was evident that my collection was entirely too big, and so I decided to split the work into two volumes. Thus, this book is Volume I.

Many of the spells come from personal grimoires that contain rituals passed down via oral tradition. Some I wrote myself. Many are derived from anthropological and archeological literature; several come from the Greek papyri and Egyptian hieroglyphics. Some are from European grimoires, and some are gleaned from slave narratives. Still others are derived from old hoodoo advertisements from the 1930s and later during the height of hoodoo commercialization. Some of the spells are based on conversations with the folks running the old Witchcraft Workshop in New Orleans many, many years ago.

In addition to these various sources, I am grateful for the contributions to this volume by Doktor Snake of *Voodoo Spellbook* fame and Carolina Dean, assistant editor for *Hoodoo and Conjure* magazine and coauthor of the *Hoodoo Almanac 2012* and *Hoodoo Almanac 2013*. I thank each of you for your generosity and creativity.

If this book, which was written mainly for popular reading, provides entertainment and a bit of education for the audience, then I have done my job.

May the warm winds of heaven blow gently on these pages and bless all who read them.

Denise Alvarado
Revised St. John's Eve, 2012

---

1. Christopher Faraone, "The Agonistic Context of Early Greek Binding Spells," in *Magika Hiera: Ancient Greek Magic and Religion,* ed. Christopher Faraone and Dirk Obbink, (New York: Oxford University Press, 1991), 3-32.

ONE

THE PIN IS MIGHTIER THAN THE SWORD

I once knew a man who spent half an hour every evening playing with a wooden doll, which was dressed to resemble a local woman who could "do things." Time after time he would thrust the little image into the fireplace until the feet touched the glowing embers, and then snatch it out again. The expression on his face was most unpleasant. I am quite indifferent to the ordinary superstitions of the hill folk. I visit graveyards at night, shoot cats on occasion, and burn sassafras wood without a tremor. And yet, something akin to horror gripped me as I watched the witch master's sadistic foolery. I should not care to have that man burning a poppet wrapped in my undershirt.[2]

If you woke up in the morning and found a little black coffin on your front porch, what would you do? Would you open it? What if you opened it and found a doll inside that had your photo attached to it?

That's exactly what happened to Commissioner Zenaida Denizac of Deltona, Florida, in the summer of 2008. As her husband headed out to her mailbox

---

2. V. Randolph, *Ozark Superstition* (London: Oxford University Press, 1947).

early one morning, he stumbled upon a black plastic dish that contained a creepy, wax-covered Voodoo doll with a photo of his wife's face attached to it. It was burned, covered in black powder, and stuck with pins all over its body.

You might say you aren't superstitious, and that you don't believe in magick and Voodoo. Commissioner Denizac did. "These are faceless cowards, people with small minds, trying to deviate me from the job I was appointed to do," Denizac said on the news. "I'm not afraid. I'm still going to speak my mind. Nothing is going to shut me up."[3]

Still, authorities considered the doll a threat to the safety and well-being of the commissioner, prompting beefed-up security and a full-blown investigation. No one believes in this Voodoo stuff, though, despite the fact that folks looked over their shoulders for a few serpents and rainbows for weeks following the incident.

Seemingly more than ever, there is a pervasive fascination with the subject of ghosts and the paranormal, haunted and cursed dolls, and things that go "bump in the night." This fascination is generally attributed to Hollywood's fusion of folklore with science fiction and the presentation of such images on the big screen. Nowhere is this more evident than with the prevailing public icon of the New Orleans Voudou religion—the Voodoo doll. The image of the pin-stuck doll is so embedded in the collective psyche of the general public that the thought of using a Voodoo doll any differently seems to defy all logic.

Hollywood and the media are not the only ones to blame for the existing attitude, however. They simply took a longstanding stereotype and ran with it. In fact, the presentation of the evil Voodoo doll began with the enslavement of African people and subsequent attempts to dehumanize them. Part of the process of dehumanization included demonizing their religions.

This book is meant to be a celebration of the ancient art of doll magick. It is true that dolls are used now, as they were in the past, in a variety of religious, spiritual, and magickal traditions. Exploring the breadth and depth of these traditions is in the very least interesting. At most it is fascinating. As you read this book, you will discover that doll magick goes far beyond sticking pins in dolls for revenge. For centuries, cultures across the globe have used the ancient techniques of image

3. "Local Commissioner Finds Voodoo Doll In Yard," *Orlando News*, http://www.wesh.com/news/16885333/detail.html.

magick, contagious magick, and sympathetic magick in combination with a doll or effigy to control all aspects of life.

Principles of Doll Magick

The various ways in which people have used dolls and effigies throughout history to control their relationships to each other, the environment, and the spiritual world are essentially based on two laws: the Law of Similarity and the Law of Contagion. Spells based on the Law of Similarity are called *sympathetic magick* or *image magick*. Image magick is based on the concept that a person can influence the well-being of another person by manipulating a doll in like fashion, i.e., *like produces like*. The most familiar application of the *like produces like* principle is injuring or destroying an enemy by virtue of injuring or destroying an image of them.[4] According to Frazer:

> For thousands of years it was known to the sorcerers of ancient India, Babylon, and Egypt, as well as of Greece and Rome, and at this day it is still resorted to by cunning and malignant savages in Australia, Africa, and Scotland. Thus the North American Indians, we are told, believe that by drawing the figure of a person in sand, ashes, or clay, or by considering any object as his body, and then pricking it with a sharp stick or doing it any other injury, they inflict a corresponding injury on the person represented. For example, when an Ojibway Indian desires to work evil on anyone, he makes a little wooden image of his enemy and runs a needle into its head or heart, or he shoots an arrow into it, believing that wherever the needle pierces or the arrow strikes the image, his foe will the same instant be seized with a sharp pain in the corresponding part of his body; but if he intends to kill the person outright, he burns or buries the puppet, uttering certain magic words as he does so. The Peruvian Indians moulded images of fat mixed with grain to imitate the persons whom they disliked or feared, and then burned the effigy on the road where the intended victim was to pass. This they called burning his soul.[5]

---

4. J. G. Frazer, *The Golden Bough: A Study in Magic and Religion* (New York: Macmillan, 1922).
5. Ibid.

According to the *Law of Contagion* (also referred to as the *Law of Contact* or *contagious magick*), once things are in contact with each other, they will continue to have an effect on each other long after they are separated.[6] Believers contend that when a personal effect, such as a fingernail, hair, or a piece of clothing, is attached to a doll, the personal effect acts as a link from the spiritual world to the physical world. Thus, the contact made between doll and personal effect allows whatever is done to the doll to happen to the person by virtue of contagion.

The spells that follow are based on both of these magickal principles. They come from a variety of ancient and contemporary traditions and are organized by category or type of spell. Many of the spells can be easily reproduced by practitioners of the occult. All of the spells are included for their folkloric and entertainment value.

A number of types of dolls are used in the various spells. In general, the spells call for dolls made of wax, clay, cloth, sticks, moss, and even store-bought dolls. I encourage you to read my book *Voodoo Dolls in Magick and Ritual* for a detailed history of doll magick and instructions for creating sticks and moss dolls, poppets, and paper Voodoo dolls. If you do not want to make your own dolls, you can use any variety of dolls at your disposal.

The spells in this book also utilize an array of herbs, roots, powders, oils, and curios, as well as images of saints, angels, talismans, psalms, and prayers. They may call for personal effects (also referred to as *taglocks*) from you or your target. Formulas for many of the special oils and powders are provided, as are the prayers and psalms. You can find all of the ingredients (sans the personal effects, of course) at your local occult supply store and at the list of suppliers in the Resources section of this book.

---

6. Ibid.

Voodoo doll from New Orleans made for the tourist trade.
From the author's private collection.

TWO

BANISHING &
UNCROSSING SPELLS

Wouldn't it be nice to be able to wiggle your nose or wave a magic wand and have your troubles instantly vanish? I always envied Samantha on *Bewitched* for her ability to make an annoying person disappear or instantly clear away the dirty dishes. And the way *I Dream of Jeannie*'s Barbara Eden could simply fold her arms and blink her eyes and whatever trouble she had accidentally conjured up would immediately vanish . . . very impressive. If only we all had genies and magick lamps.

Well, maybe we can't make unwanted people, places, and things disappear by wiggling our noses or blinking our eyes, but we can get rid of unwanted influences in our lives. When we align with universal forces and direct energy where we want it to go, we reclaim our personal power and become cocreators of our lives rather than passive recipients. As Maya Angelou once said, "If you don't like something, change it." To change something, we must take action. And so it is with magick; it is an action-oriented approach to life, a way to master one's own fate.

The magickal act of driving away negativity and evil is called *banishment*. Banishing spells are designed to get rid of illnesses, negative emotions, and conditions. They function to block negative thoughtforms that may be directed towards you. They are excellent for exorcising undesirable spirits, entities, and demons that may be lingering within the home or that may have been sent there to work against you. And whether you are under verbal, emotional, or physical attack, or have an annoying neighbor, jilted lover, jealous friend, or an abusive boyfriend, a good old-fashioned Enemy Be Gone spell can do wonders.

Although banishing spells can be performed at any time, occultists advise that pracitioners perform banishing spells on Sundays under a waning moon or full moon while facing west. It is usually a good idea to follow a banishing spell with a spell of protection or cleansing bath so you have spiritual defenses in place to prevent the negativity from returning.

Uncrossing spells are those that are intended to reverse the effects of a negative spiritual attack, which is referred to as being "crossed" in hoodoo. When you uncross a person, you are restoring that person to his or her natural state of being. You are cleansing that person of negativity so that any bad luck or illness that they experience as a result of being crossed is removed.

Bottle Spell to Make a Person Move

This spell is part of a longstanding hoodoo tradition, the bottle spell. Bottle spells have their origin in a tradition that was brought over to the New World by enslaved Africans from the Congo region.

In Africa, cobalt-blue bottles were hung at the entrances of homes or in nearby trees as talismans to capture evil spirits. The spirits are said to be mesmerized by the colors of the bottle; once inside, they cannot escape. Just like cats cannot resist catnip, evil spirits find the beautiful blue-colored bottles and the rays of sunlight dancing through them irresistible.

Once in the New World, the bottle-as-talisman took on different forms. Much like the witch's bottles that can be traced to the 1600s, bottles began to be used in spellwork. Bottles of all colors, shapes, and sizes were filled with herbs and other items of significance for the purpose of protection, repelling evil, or attracting luck. Eventually, the bottle spell became a fundamental element of hoodoo magick.

The following spell is designed to make someone move. You will need a wide-mouth jar or bottle that will hold a doll baby. You will also need the following items:

Sea salt
Purple fabric
Garlic
Red pepper
Graveyard dirt
Brown paper bag
Black pin

Take the jar and wash it with sea salt. Create a doll baby out of purple fabric and stuff it with garlic, red pepper, and graveyard dirt. Tear a piece of paper from a brown paper bag, write your target's name and birth date (if you know it) on the paper, and attach it to the doll baby with a black pin. Stuff the doll baby inside the jar and urinate on it, filling up the jar as much as possible. Put the top on the jar and throw it into a body of running water, visualizing your enemy moving away from you as you do this.

Marie Laveaux Banishing Doll Ritual

Here is a simple banishing spell that is believed to have originated with Marie Laveaux, the infamous Voodoo Queen of New Orleans.

Marie Laveaux's bottle spell is simple, yet it is a classic of New Orleans hoo-doo. For this spell you will need:

Bottle
Four Thieves vinegar
Parchment paper
Small doll made from black cloth, or store-bought doll dressed in black

On a piece of parchment paper, write the name of the person you want to leave. Attach it to the doll and stuff the doll into the bottle. Fill the bottle with Four Thieves vinegar and seal it. Throw the bottle into the Mississippi River or any moving body of water. According to legend, Marie Laveaux asserts that as the bottle is carried away by the water, so shall this person be removed from your location.

Formula for Four Thieves Vinegar

Rosemary tops, dried, 4 oz.
Sage flowers, dried, 4 oz.
Lavender flowers, dried, 2 oz.
Rue, fresh, 1 ½ oz.
Camphor, dissolved in spirit, 1 oz.
Garlic, sliced, ¼ oz.
Cloves, bruised, 1 drm
Distilled wine vinegar, strongest, 1 gal.

Digest for seven or eight days, with occasional agitation. Pour off the liquor, press out the remainder, and filter the mixed liquids. It is said that this medicated vinegar was invented by four thieves of Marseilles, who successfully employed it as a prophylactic during a visitation of pestilence.[7]

Poppet to Banish Illness

Here is a Wiccan spell designed to heal someone who is sick by using a poppet that represents them. Gather the following items:

Poppet made from white fabric
Angelica root, cut and sifted
Gold coin
Peppermint
Basil
Red wine
Wine glass

Create a poppet out of white fabric that has been soaked in a tea made from Angelica root. Place a gold coin inside the poppet and stuff with peppermint and basil. Name the poppet for the person who is ill. To name your poppet, simply say "As I have made you, so shall you be named [state the person's name]." Place the poppet

---

7. Albert Allis Hopkins, ed., *The Scientific American Cyclopedia of Receipts, Notes and Queries* (New York: Munn & Co., 1901).

in a full glass of red wine under a waning moon for three nights. Each night, drink a third of the wine that has not been absorbed by the poppet. On the third night, throw the poppet into a running body of water, forcing the illness to leave the afflicted.

St. Expedite Spell to Get Rid of a Person

Saint Expedite is the patron saint of those who need fast solutions to problems, who strive to put an end to procrastination and delays, and who seek financial success. His feast day is April 19th. In Haitian Voodoo, Baron La Croix is often represented by St. Expedite. In New Orleans Voodoo, he is associated with Baron Samedi, the spirit of death.

According to a legend, Saint Expeditus was a Roman centurion in Armenia who was beheaded during the Diocletian Persecution in 303 AD. On the day he decided to become a Christian, the Devil took the form of a crow or a snake and told him to postpone his conversion until the next day. Instead, Expeditus stomped on the animal and killed it, proclaiming, "I'll be a Christian today!"

In New Orleans hoodoo, it is customary to offer St. Expedite pound cake, flowers, and a glass of water. He is believed to grant any request within his power, provided the petitioner recommends his invocation to others. In this tradition, his image in the form of holy cards and medals is used in gambling charms and crossing rituals.

This spell seeks the assistance of St. Expedite. Perform this spell on a Friday. Write the name of your target on a red balloon filled with helium. Make a very small Voodoo doll out of red fabric, anoint it with Fast Luck oil or St. Expedite oil, and attach a medal of St. Expedite to the doll. Light a red candle. Place a holy card of St. Expedite on your altar and offer him a glass of water. Say the following prayer:

Saint Expedite, you lay in rest.
I come to you and ask that this wish be granted.
_____ [Express exactly what you want, and ask him to find a
    way to get it to you.]
Expedite now what I ask of you.
Expedite now what I want of you, this very second.

Don't waste another day.
Grant me what I ask for.
I know your power, I know you because of your work.
I know you can help me.
Do this for me and I will spread your name with love and honor
*   so that it will be invoked again and again.*
Expedite this wish with speed, love, honor, and goodness.
Glory to you, Saint Expedite!

Tie the balloon to the Voodoo doll and release into the air. The person should leave in whatever direction the wind is blowing. When your request is granted, thank St. Expedite by offering him a piece of Sara Lee pound cake. Offering Sara Lee pound cake is customary in New Orleans, but if you do not have the Sara Lee brand, use what you have. You should also thank him publicly to let others know of his generosity. If you do not thank him in this manner, he will take back your request and then some, so be sure to remember this step.

Saint Expedite with his typical iconographical attributes.

Banish a Woman Who Is Trying to Steal Your Man

If another woman is trying to steal your man, try this simple but potentially disgusting banishing spell to eliminate the competition. Create a black doll baby and stuff it with Spanish moss, devil's dung (Asafoetida), and sulphur. Write the other woman's name on parchment paper and attach the name paper to the doll with a black pin. Put the doll in the stinkiest, filthiest place you can think of (such as a garbage dump, sewer, or outdoor toilet) and tell the doll what you think of her and what you want her to do. Then, leave the place and do not look back. In no time, the woman will be so uncomfortable with her home and job that she will move.

SPANISH MOSS

Spanish moss has several magickal correspondences. It is a traditional filler for Voodoo dolls and doll babies, and is essentially neutral until it is charged with specific intent. In New Orleans, it became staple paraphernalia of conjure due to its availability. Spanish moss is excellent for crossings due to its epiphytic nature, meaning it is considered parasitic because it lives off the trees in which it is found. If you consider the concept of the doctrine of signatures, then you can use Spanish moss to "smother" someone, or stunt someone's growth (spiritually, physically, emotionally, or mentally) as this is something Spanish moss does naturally in relation to the tree it inhabits. It is also a natural habitat for animals such as bats and spiders and can intrinsically possess some strong jinxing qualities, if so energized.

Get Rid of a Troubling Ex-Lover

If you have broken up with your ex but they just won't let you go; if they keep calling you even when you tell them to stop; or if they harass you or are stalking you, then try this doll spell to get rid of them. For this spell you will need:

A wide-mouth jar
A black doll baby that can fit inside the jar
Personal effect of your ex
Brown paper bag

Dragon's Blood ink
Black pin
Photo
Black witch's salt
Red pepper
Graveyard dirt
Lost and Away powder

Attach a personal effect from your ex to the doll with a black pin. Write down their name and date of birth on a piece of brown paper bag with Dragon's Blood ink and attach it to the doll. If you have a photo of this person, attach it to the doll. Stick the doll into the jar and add some black witch's salt, red pepper, graveyard dirt, and Lost and Away powder. Seal the jar shut and throw into a running river. If it is carried away from you, you can expect the person to leave you alone within nine days. If it sinks to the bottom or is carried towards you, then you must repeat the spell, this time burning a black candle on top of the jar for nine days. You should inscribe the person's name on the candle and roll the candle with Lost and Away powder before burning. After burning the candle for nine days, take it to the river again and throw it in. If you still do not have any luck getting rid of the person and the person is stalking or otherwise harassing you, take out a restraining order and repeat the spell during a waning moon.

Formula for Lost and Away Powder

Dirt from a crossroads
Mistletoe
Powdered sulfur
Powdered orris root
Sage

Grind the dried herbs with a mortar and pestle until they are a fine powder. Then mix the powder with the graveyard dirt and powdered sulphur.

To Make a Person Move

Here is an old Southern hoodoo spell that uses the infamous New Orleans black coffin. Take a twenty-inch by twenty-inch piece of red flannel and tie a foot of a dead animal to each corner. Make a black Voodoo doll or buy a doll and dress it in black and attach a taglock to the doll. A taglock can be a photo or personal item that belongs to your enemy. Place the doll in a small coffin or box painted black that can function as a coffin. Grab some powdered sulphur and take it, the cloth, and the coffin with the doll inside over to the home of your enemy. Discreetly lay out the cloth on your enemy's doorstep and make a cross in the center with the powdered sulphur. Put the coffin with the doll inside on top of the sulphur. Do not close the coffin. When your enemy opens the door and sees this work, he or she will surely leave.

Traditional New Orleans Coffin Spell

Here is another variation of the traditional New Orleans Voodoo doll coffin spell. Perform this spell during a waning moon to remove an enemy from your life. This spell is also good for transformative magick, where the doll symbolizes the transformation of something negative into something positive, or the death of something old into something new.

This spell requires quite a few items. You will need:

Plate
Crucifix
Fiery Wall of Protection oil
Angelica root
Fiery Wall of Protection sachet powder
St. Michael the Archangel holy card
7 purple offertory candles
1 white candle
Graveyard dirt
Black pin
Parchment paper
Small black coffin

Clean white cloth
Twine
9 pennies
Small bottle of rum

Lay a cross in front of the plate and anoint with the Fiery Wall of Protection oil. Dress the Angelica root with the Fiery Wall of Protection oil as well. Lay a circle of protection around the cross and Angelica root with the Fiery Wall of Protection sachet powder. As you are dressing the cross and the Angelica root, repeat the following:

Saint Michael the Archangel, protect me and defend me in battle.

When you are done preparing the cross and Angelica root, lay the St. Michael the Archangel holy card in the center of the circle and sprinkle with a little Fiery Wall of Protection powder. Place the white candle in the circle. Then, take the seven purple offertory candles and inscribe the names of seven people, angels, saints, or spirits who represent your personal army of protection on the candles; write one name per candle. Anoint the candles with the Fiery Wall of Protection oil and roll in the sachet powder. Set the candles on the circle of protection around the cross, Angelica root, and St. Michael the Archangel holy card. Sprinkle a bit more of the Fiery Wall of Protection sachet powder on the St. Michael the Archangel holy card, cross, and Angelica root.

Place the graveyard dirt in a fireproof dinner plate. Attach a photo of your target to the Voodoo doll with a black pin and write your target's name nine times on a piece of parchment paper. On top of and crossing the person's name, write nine power words that describe your feelings for this person, such as *wicked, evil, hate, sick,* and so on. Attach the name paper to the doll with a black pin. Lay the doll on the graveyard dirt in the plate. Place the plate to the left of the circle. Do not put the doll and plate inside your circle of protection.

Begin lighting the purple candles going clockwise. Light the white candle next. Repeat the following prayer:

Saint Michael the Archangel, defend me in battle.
Be my protection against the wickedness and snares of the devil.
May God rebuke him, I humbly pray;
and do Thou, O Prince of the Heavenly Host,
by the Divine Power of God,
cast into hell, Satan, and all the evil spirits,
who roam throughout the world seeking the ruin of souls. Amen.

Now, speak a heartfelt prayer of your own, asking your spiritual army led by St. Michael the Archangel for protection and divine assistance with the expulsion of your enemy. Then, light the black Voodoo doll on fire. As it burns, say:

Your evil is returned!
Your evil is undone!
Your evil is done!
You are done!

Let the doll burn out in the fireproof dish. When it is extinguished, place the graveyard dirt and the remains of the doll inside the black coffin.

Take the cross, Angelica root, and St. Michael the Archangel holy card and wrap in the clean white cloth. Anoint with Fiery Wall of Protection oil and sprinkle with Fiery Wall of Protection powder. Tie it closed with seven knots to represent your Divine Army of Seven. Hang it behind your front door for protection. You can also carry it with you as a protective talisman.

Take the coffin with the remains and the plate and go to one of the forty-two Cities of the Dead (New Orleans cemeteries). Find a tomb with a cross and bury the coffin under the tree closest to the grave. Then, take the dish and throw it as hard as you can against the wall of the tomb, breaking the plate. Leave nine pennies and a small bottle of rum at the cemetery gates as you leave to appease the spirits. Turn around and leave the cemetery and never return to that spot. If you do not live in New Orleans, you can go to any cemetery and find any grave with a cross to use to finalize this spell.

Formula for Fiery Wall of Protection Oil

Use the essential oils or essences for the ingredients listed. The dried herbs can be used in place of oil or as an adjunct to the oil.

Frankincense
Dragon's blood resin
Rue
Salt
Ginger essential oil
Cayenne pepper
Bay essential oil

Blend equal amounts of the above ingredients to a base of olive oil that has a small amount of vitamin E added to it as a preservative.

Reverse a Curse Poppet Spell

This spell uses the most ancient technique of image magick because it involves a doll that represents the spirit of a person who has placed a curse on you. Create a poppet that is red on one side and black on the other. The red represents your power and the black is for repelling the curse. Write the name of your enemy on a piece of parchment paper and attach it to the black side of the doll. Hold the doll and begin to rock back and forth to get into a trance-like state. Repeat the following chant as if it were a mantra: "The curse is broken, I take back my power. The spell is undone, the curse is gone. My power is returned to me as the curse returns to you threefold. Your power is no more." When the chant is complete, burn some sage and take a cleansing bath. To take a cleansing bath, add a cup of sea salt and pray Psalm 23 over it. Then, add it to your bath water and soak for fifteen minutes. Concentrate on the positive influences entering your life. Repeat the ritual for seven consecutive days. On the seventh day, take the doll to a crossroads and leave it there with three pennies.

Break a Curse

If you feel you have become the target of someone else's wrath or vengeance, create a poppet to represent the one who has cast the curse. Place the poppet in a box and bury it under a thin layer of soil. Directly above where you buried the poppet, light a bonfire and chant your wish that the curse cast against you will be consumed along with the flames that burn the poppet lying in the shallow grave below.[8]

Uncrossing and Protection Doll

For this uncrossing spell, you will need white fabric with a loose weave that has been washed in Essence of Van Van. Allow the fabric to air dry. Then, create a doll baby and stuff it with bird seed, powdered cinnamon, brown sugar, and powdered High John the Conqueror root. Sew the doll baby closed. Light a white vigil candle and for nine days pray Psalm 40 while holding the doll close to your body. After the ninth day, plant the doll in a shallow hole in a sunny place in your yard. Cover with about a half an inch of fertile soil. Every day before noon, water the doll baby and pray Psalm 54 over the spot where you have planted your spell (be careful not to overwater). Soon you will see the seeds grow; as they grow, so shall the uncrossing grow. Once the seeds are fully grown, the spell is complete, your prayers have been answered, and the uncrossing is done.

Formula for Essence of Van Van

Lemongrass
Palmarosa
Vetivert
Grain alcohol (Everclear)

Combine thirteen drops each of the above oils to half a cup of grain alcohol.

---

8. A. Pustanio, "Voodoo Doll Haunted America Tours," http://www.hauntedamericatours.com/voodoo/voodoodolls/voodoodoll/.

Psalm 40

I waited patiently for the LORD; and he inclined unto me, and heard my cry.

He brought me up also out of an horrible pit, out of the miry clay, and set my feet upon a rock, and established my goings.

And he hath put a new song in my mouth, even praise unto our God: many shall see it, and fear, and shall trust in the LORD.

Blessed is that man that maketh the LORD his trust, and respecteth not the proud, nor such as turn aside to lies.

Many, O LORD my God, are thy wonderful works which thou hast done, and thy thoughts which are to us-ward: they cannot be reckoned up in order unto thee: if I would declare and speak of them, they are more than can be numbered.

Sacrifice and offering thou didst not desire; mine ears hast thou opened: burnt offering and sin offering hast thou not required.

Then said I, Lo, I come: in the volume of the book it is written of me,

I delight to do thy will, O my God: yea, thy law is within my heart.

I have preached righteousness in the great congregation: lo, I have not re-frained my lips, O LORD, thou knowest.

I have not hid thy righteousness within my heart; I have declared thy faithful-ness and thy salvation: I have not concealed thy lovingkindness and thy truth from the great congregation.

Withhold not thou thy tender mercies from me, O LORD: let thy lovingkind-ness and thy truth continually preserve me.

For innumerable evils have compassed me about: mine iniquities have taken hold upon me, so that I am not able to look up; they are more than the hairs of mine head: therefore my heart faileth me.

Be pleased, O LORD, to deliver me: O LORD, make haste to help me.

Let them be ashamed and confounded together that seek after my soul to destroy it; let them be driven backward and put to shame that wish me evil.

Let them be desolate for a reward of their shame that say unto me, Aha, aha.

Let all those that seek thee rejoice and be glad in thee: let such as love thy salva-tion say continually, The LORD be magnified.

But I am poor and needy; yet the Lord thinketh upon me: thou art my help and my deliverer; make no tarrying, O my God.[9]

Psalm 54

Save me, O God, by thy name, and judge me by thy strength.
Hear my prayer, O God; give ear to the words of my mouth.
For strangers are risen up against me, and oppressors seek after my soul: they have not set God before them. Selah.
Behold, God is mine helper: the Lord is with them that uphold my soul.
He shall reward evil unto mine enemies: cut them off in thy truth.
I will freely sacrifice unto thee: I will praise thy name, O LORD; for it is good.
For he hath delivered me out of all trouble: and mine eye hath seen his desire upon mine enemies.[10]

Shall we write about the things not to be spoken of?
Shall we divulge the things not to be divulged?
Shall we pronounce the things not to be pronounced?

Julian, Hymn to the Mother of the Gods

---

9. Scripture quotations taken from the 21st Century King James Version, copyright 1994. Used by permission of Deuel Enterprises, Inc., Gary, SD 57237. All rights reserved.
10. Scripture quotations taken from the 21st Century King James Version, copyright 1994. Used by permission of Deuel Enterprises, Inc., Gary, SD 57237. All rights reserved.

THREE

CURSES, HEXES & SPELLS FOR REVENGE

Hexing, cursing, and jinxing are activities that are considered by many occultists to be left-handed magick. Aside from love spells, curses are what Voodoo dolls are best known for. Curses also instill fear into the minds of many, and with good reason. There is a strong psychological component to the idea of someone surreptitiously sticking pins into a doll with the intent of causing harm or misfortune. Just the suggestion of someone hexing you with a Voodoo doll is enough to create a self-fulfilling prophecy. In other words, if you believe things will go wrong, they often will.

A curse is the effective action of some power, or the result from a spell or prayer, asking that a god, natural force, or spirit bring misfortune to someone. Curses and hexes are considered black magic spells because they are concerned with hurting and harming a person. In hoodoo, curses are referred to as goofering, jinxing, or hot-footing an enemy. On the other hand, certain types of spells can be used to repel negative energy, keep a perpetrator from hurting someone, or drive away bad neighbors.[11]

---

11. "Banish, Bind, and Enemy Be Gone: The Anatomy of the Voodoo Curse," http://www.squidoo.com/voodoocurses.

In New Orleans, it is said that burning black candles on a person will bring about a slow death or harm, depending on your intention. Red candles, on the other hand, are said to bring about swift harm attributed to an accident of some sort.[12]

Ancient Spell to Inflict Pain

King George IV's wife, Caroline of Brunswick, was accused of being a witch because he suffered from a chronic pain condition. She famously accused him of neglecting her and he assumed that in revenge she had made a wax doll of him in order to inflict pain.[13] Apparently, she was not happy with her marriage and spent many hours forming wax dolls of her husband and jabbing them with pins. Although history gives us no direct evidence as to the effect this may have had on King George IV, when his wife ran off to a villa in Italy to live with her Italian lover, King George didn't protest. The royal couple remained married but lived separately until Caroline's death in 1821.

This spell uses the same technique that Caroline of Brunswick used to inflict pain upon her husband. To make a wax poppet, coat your hands with a few drops of an essential oil or conjure oil consistent with the intent of your work, and mold a shape out of softened wax. You can mix hair or nail clippings or some other personal effect of the intended recipient into the wax figure. Carve the name of your enemy onto the poppet nine times with a nail. Then stick the wax doll with pins while cursing it. When done, throw the wax doll into a fire and watch it melt away.

Avenge a Scorned Love

This is a spell based on old New Orleans traditional witchcraft principles. Back in the 1970s, there was a little witchcraft and gris gris shop in the French Quarter called the *Witches Workshop* that I used to frequent for supplies. It was one of my favorite places to visit when I was down in the French Quarter, which was nearly every weekend. I loved the way it smelled; the atmosphere was all dark and haunted, but something about the atmosphere was so alluring. It was owned and operated by the well-respected Witch Queen Mary Oneida Toups, a High Priestess

12. J. Haskins, *Voodoo & Hoodoo* (London: Scarborough House, 1990).
13. "Famous Witches," http://socyberty.com/folklore/famous-witches/.

of the Religious Order of Witchcraft in New Orleans and author of *Magick, High and Low*. I was just a teenager at the time, but the memories I have of that place will stay with me forever.

Oneida Toups is surrounded by the mystery and fascination of any great legend and many are said to have known her. Early in the 1970s, she and her husband Boots Toups got together with Dr. John and formed the Dr. John Temple of Voodoo out of that famous shop on St. Phillips Street. In my mind, it was the best place ever after that happened. I have always been a huge fan of Dr. John and though I was quite shy at the time and too scared to approach him, I distinctly remember being in his presence on a number of occasions. I could just feel the gris gris grooving in that man's veins. That is one magickal cat. But I digress. . . .

Maybe it was because I was so young, but the folks there were quite friendly to me and greeted me with a secret greeting every time I walked in. They would give recommendations for things I thought I needed; in truth, I was just going there because it was such a cool place to go and it really didn't matter what I walked out with. Just the fact that I got to go there was enough for me.

Once I went down to that little gris gris shop with a purpose in mind. A friend's father had been attacked by a satanist we knew who fancied one or both of us. My friend's father didn't care for the fact that his daughter was hanging out with a satanist, much less an older man. He was in his twenties and we were about thirteen at the time. It was fun hanging out with him and he was teaching us about witchcraft. Nothing funny went on between us, but her dad didn't know that. So he told her she couldn't hang out with him anymore. That killed my friend, as she was quite smitten with this guy.

The next day, my friend's father walked out of his house and saw a large pentagram with a black skull candle burning in the center of it etched on the street. There was some sinister message that accompanied the pentagram, but I don't remember what it was.

To make matters worse, this guy wouldn't talk to my friend anymore, driving by her house and taunting her, saying mean things and really hurting her feelings. So, I had to take matters into my own hands. She was my best friend, after all.

I explained the situation to the folks down at the gris gris shop and they told me to remember one of witchcraft's oldest teachings: *Don't get mad, get even*. Then, they anointed a red candle for me in oils and rolled it in some special herbs, then wrapped it up in some plastic wrap and gave it to me with the following instructions.

To make sure that a mean lover suffers three times the agony he has caused you, light a red candle on a night when you are feeling particularly heartbroken. Stare intently at the flame as it flickers, and remember how miserable this man has made you. Then, make a Voodoo moss doll to represent the guy while you are feeling these powerful emotions. To do so, grab a couple of sticks and tie them in a cross shape. Take some Spanish moss and wrap it around the sticks, then wrap the doll in a piece of this guy's clothing. If you have some hair or fingernails, stick those inside the doll and wrap the fabric around it, sealing it in. Tie everything in place with a piece of yarn or string. Take a straw and put it where the mouth of the doll would be and breathe into the doll through the straw. This will activate the doll, as you are symbolically *breathing life* into the doll. Then, name the doll after the person it represents.

Next, take some pins and stick the doll wherever you want, but each time say, *I hate you, you hurt me!* Do this as many times as you need to. Then, take the candle carefully, and as it still burns allow the wax to drip on the doll where the pins are stuck, sealing the pins in place, and say, *You burned me and now I burn you!* Put the candle back down in the holder and allow it to continue to burning. Pick up the doll and touch the head to the candle flame, just enough to let it singe, and say, *You think you are so smart, now you are stupid and confused!* Turn the doll around and singe the bottom of the doll with the candle flame and say, *Burn and fall like Icarus from the sun!* The singeing of the head and feet should continue until the candle is burned down or until you have had enough. When finished, the doll and the wax remains should be placed in a paper bag and thrown into the Mississippi River.

Once this is done, you should not ever hear from the person again. Come to think of it, we never did hear from that guy again. . . .

Black Arts Spell

Make a Voodoo doll out of black cloth to represent your enemy. Anoint the doll with Black Arts oil. Burn a black candle for seventeen minutes each day for nine days. Hold the candle over the doll, allowing the wax to drip on the doll. While you are doing this, curse at the doll as if it were your enemy. Say every nasty thing you ever wanted to say, yell, or scream. After the ninth day, place the remainder of the candle along with the doll in a small box. Wrap the box in black cloth; using twine, tie it closed with nine knots. Take the box to the cemetery and bury it. Pay the spirits of the cemetery nine pennies and a small bottle of rum. Walk away without looking back.

Formula for Black Arts Oil

Use the essential oils or essences for the ingredients listed. The dried herbs can be used in place of oil or as an adjunct to the oil.

Pinch of mullein
Pinch of graveyard dirt
Patchouli essential oil
9 black peppercorns
Pinch of powdered sulphur
Spanish moss
Vetivert
Ghost chilies

Mix the above ingredients in a base of mineral oil.

Black Pin Spell

For your classic, stereotypical Voodoo doll curse, try this spell. To make your Voodoo doll represent a person, place some of that person's hair or a personal item inside the cloth of the doll to capture part of their soul. Stick a black pin into the part of the body where you want the person to experience pain. For example, a pin in the heart can cause heartbreak or heart problems, a pin in the stomach a stomachache, a pin in the back a backache or relationship problems, and so on. With each stick you must focus your intention with the utmost clarity. Then, place the doll on the person's doorstep or in their mailbox and watch them totally freak out. Or, bury it in your enemy's yard at midnight.

Feather Fetish to Make a Person Sick

For this spell, you will need a bunch of colorful feathers and some black thread. Take a handful of colorful feathers similar in length and tie them together with the twine. Take another bunch of colorful feathers that are about a quarter inch shorter in length than the first bunch and tie them together. You should now have two bound bunches of feathers. Tie the two bunches together in a cross position. It should now resemble a crude human form. Wind the thread around the figure several times to securely hold the feathers in place. There are two ways you can use this doll: you can place the feather doll inside the pillow of your enemy and they will suffer horrible headaches; or you can slowly unwind the thread over a period of nine days and when the doll falls apart, so will your victim.

Spell for a Curse That Only You Can Remove

This is a curse from Louisiana. Interestingly, it is one I did many moons ago with great success. It is not one that was taught to me by anyone, but one that just came to me during a fit of rage after someone ripped me off. To my surprise, I while I was doing research for this book I came across a similar spell that was told by an informant in New Iberia, Louisiana. This is their version.

Use a black candle, the three of spades from a deck of cards, and a Voodoo doll. Utter the curse as you place your victim's likeness on the doll. Burn the black candle and place the three of spades face up on the doll.[14]

Now here is my version of a similar spell: Use a black candle, a jack of spades, a Voodoo doll, and black thread. Light the black candle and let it burn. Write your enemy's name on the playing card. Place the jack of spades face up on the doll and wrap the doll and the card together with the black thread as you utter your curse. The words you speak must come from a place of extreme anger and you must be extremely focused. Bury the doll away from your home in the direction of your enemy's home.

The person who ripped me off and for whom I performed this spell was dragged down the street by a car and suffered a broken arm and dislocated shoulder the following day. Well, he really pissed me off. . . .

---

14. R. Bodin, *Voodoo Past and Present* (Lafayette, Louisiana: University of Southwestern Louisiana, 1990).

Stick It to Your Enemy

This is another spell that is Southern hoodoo in origin. Make a doll baby out of black fabric. Write the name of your enemy on a piece of brown paper. Pierce the paper with a black pin into the doll in the area corresponding to your enemy's body part on which you wish to inflict pain. Once pierced, wrap the doll in a shroud of white gauze and pray over it as if it were a deceased person. When the death rites have been accomplished, bury the doll in a spot over which your enemy is sure to walk.

THE MELTING OF WAX DOLLS IN THE FOUNDATION DECREE OF CYREA

Oaths were sworn to this agreement both by those who remained in Thera and those who sailed to settle. And they called down curses on those who should foreswear themselves and fail to abide by the oath, be they among those settling in Libya or those remaining behind in Thera. They molded wax dolls [Kolossoi] and burned them while falling down the curse, all having come together, men, women, boys, and girls. They prayed that the one that did not abide by the oaths but foreswore himself should melt and dissolve just like the dolls, he himself, the descendents, and his property, but that those that did abide by these oaths whether among those sailing to Libya or remaining behind in Thera, should have many good things, both they themselves and their descendents (Greek iv. B.C.)[15]

15. R. Meiggs, *A Selection of Greek Historical Inscriptions* (Oxford, UK: Oxford University Press, 1969).

Georgia Witch Salt Dough Doll Baby

If there is someone causing mischief and mayhem in your life, try making this Georgia witch salt dough doll baby. To make this doll baby, you will have to make a batch of salt dough. You will have quite a bit of extra dough, but it will store for several months in the refrigerator so you can have some on hand for future conjurings. To make a doll baby out of salt dough, try the following foolproof recipe.

Doll Baby Salt Dough

2 cups water
3 tablespoons vegetable oil
2 ½ cups flour
½ cups black witch's salt
Handful of mullein

The night before you make this dough, you will need to steep a handful of mullein in the water overnight. In the morning, strain the herbs from the water. Pour the water into a pot and bring it to a boil. Add vegetable oil. Allow to cool just slightly, so that the water is still warm. Add the flour and black witch's salt and mix well. The dough should be warm, soft, and pliable.

Take a small amount of dried mullein and pulverize it into a fine powder using a coffee grinder or mortar and pestle. When it is cool, work the clay with your hands. Carefully add a teaspoon of the powdered mullein to some of the clay you have just made and mix well. Fashion an image of a man or woman (the gender should match that of your enemy). While working the dough, repeat the bothersome person's name over and over again, directing the person to stop meddling in your affairs. Take some thorns from a honey locust and stick them into the doll wherever you see fit. You can substitute pins, nails, or cactus thorns if you do not have access to honey locust thorns. Place the doll on a piece of wax paper and allow it to dry. Drying time will vary according to the size of the doll, but it should be dry within a couple of hours. Bury the doll in your enemy's yard and it should quickly take effect. After one year, you should make another doll in like fashion to continue the influence.

The extra doll baby dough should be stored in an airtight container. You can fix the dough by adding any kind of herb in the same fashion as has been described, using herbs that are consistent with the purpose of the spell to be performed. This can be the foundation for any number of conjure dolls needed for spells in this book.

Get Even Gris Gris Doll

Here's a creepy little revenge spell. Create a small doll baby out of black fabric. Stuff the doll with saffron, salt, gunpowder, graveyard dirt, powdered dog manure, and crumpled newspaper from the obituary section. Place the doll near your enemy—under their front porch, in their dresser drawer, in their purse, in the kitchen cabinets. Be sure to be discreet. They will surely suffer three times the anguish they have caused you.

Keep a Person Frustrated and Unsuccessful

The following spell was provided by an informant in Jim Haskin's book, *Voodoo and Hoodoo*. It is designed to sabotage the success and happiness of an enemy. I have included it here because I have in my collection a vintage doll that is constructed in a similar fashion as the one described. The back of the doll has a slit into which there is a petition paper stuffed, and it could easily be positioned in the way the informant describes. I did not remove the paper because it is part of the collection for the Voodoo Doll Museum and I don't want to tamper with its historical value. Here is the description of a doll as provided by Haskin's informant:

> *Write the name of the victim on parchment paper. Make a slit in the back of a doll made of black cloth and put the paper in it. Put cayenne pepper in the slit with the paper and sew up the doll with black thread. Tie the doll's hands at the back and place it in a kneeling position in a corner that is untrafficked. As long as the doll is undisturbed, the person represented will be "kept down." You may subject it to other indignities—kick it, blindfold it. Corresponding problems will befall the victim.*[16]

---

16. Haskins, *Voodoo & Hoodoo*.

Vintage Voodoo doll with slit in the back stuffed with a petition paper.

Heartburn Revenge Doll

This spell is designed to get back at the person who has broken your heart. Make a black Voodoo moss doll and stick the heart area full of pins. Skewer it through the heart region and set it to roast before a fire, while singing with a group of your friends:

> *It is not this heart I mean to burn.*
> *But the person's heart I wish to turn,*
> *Wishing them neither rest nor peace*
> *Till they are dead and gone.*

Take turns sprinkling salt over the burning doll and telling it what you think. Say everything you have ever wanted to say to the person who has broken your heart. Continue in this fashion until the doll has been burnt to a crisp and nothing but ashes remain.

THE VOODOO DOLL SPELLBOOK

Hex Your Enemy Ritual

Perform this ritual when you want bad luck and chaos to follow your enemy. Make a Voodoo doll out of black fabric. With a red paint pen, write the name of your enemy on the doll. Lightly stuff the doll with sulfur, graveyard dirt, and Spanish moss.

Thread a needle with red thread and stick it in the head of the doll. Sew the thread in and out all the way down to the feet and pull the thread tightly but carefully so it doesn't break. This will cause the doll to gather and become disfigured and small. Place the doll in a small box and take it to a cemetery. Dig a small hole and place the box in the hole. Place some Devil's Shoestring on top of the box and sprinkle with Black Arts oil. Then cover the box with the graveyard dirt. As you are covering the box, state what misfortune you would have befall your enemy. When the box is completely covered, say "Let it be so." Leave the cemetery and never return to where the box was buried.

Hillbilly's Revenge Bone Wax Doll

This Voodoo doll is good for when you have a lot of anger and rage towards someone because it provides a means of expression and release. This Voodoo doll spell draws on the principles of sympathetic magick to create long-lasting health problems for the intended victim by using bone wax to create a representative effigy of a target.

For this spell you will need to procure some beeswax and transform it into bone wax. Beeswax was the first "plastic" used in antiquity, and for thousands of years has been used as a modeling material, to create sculpture and jewelry molds, and for making little effigies in human form for magickal works. When combined with a softening agent like paraffin or olive oil, it is known as bone wax. Bone wax was once used to stop bone bleeding during surgical procedures. When used in a medical setting, bone wax increases infection rates, impairs the ability of bone to clear bacteria, and can inhibit bone tissue formation.

Make some bone wax by melting beeswax with paraffin. Allow to cool until malleable. Create a wax effigy in the likeness of your enemy. Concentrate on how they hurt you—act it out on the effigy. For example, if your heart is broken, take a nail and dig out the heart of the effigy. Say something to this effect: *I send my broken heart back to you. Now your heart is broken and empty, not mine.* If the person stole from you, take a knife and cut off the hands of the effigy. Say something to this effect: *You will steal no longer.* Slowly dismember the effigy until you have a pile of wax pieces. Then, squeeze the pile of wax together into a ball, and toss into a can of dirty motor oil. Pray Psalm 23 backwards three times and your enemy will suffer three times the amount of agony they caused you.

Malay Charm to Scorch the Soul of an Enemy

Here is a spell from *The Golden Bough* that the author Sir James George Frazer describes as an illustration of homeopathic or imitative magic.

Take parings of nails, hair, eyebrows, spittle, and so forth of your intended victim, enough to represent every part of his person, and then make them up into his likeness with wax from a deserted bees' comb. Scorch the figure slowly by holding it over a lamp every night for seven nights, and say:

> *It is not wax that I am scorching,*
> *It is the liver, heart, and spleen of So-and-so that I scorch.*

After the seventh day, burn the waxen image and your victim will die. According to Frazer, this spell falls into the category of homeopathic or imitative magic because the waxen image is made in the likeness of the enemy and contains personal effects that were once in contact with them.[18]

Hot Foot Hannibal Conjure Doll

This conjure doll spell comes from one of seven stories in *The Conjure Woman* by Charles Waddell Chesnutt. In this story, a slave woman creates a conjure doll in order to unite with the man she loves rather than the house slave her master chooses for her. It can be hard to read because it was written phonetically according to Southern black dialect, but here is an excerpt that deals with the conjure doll followed by my interpretation and version of the spell:

---

17. Footnote to come.
18. Frazer, *The Golden Bough.*

So de nex' night Jeff went back, en Aun' Peggy gun "im a baby-doll, wid a body made out'n a piece er co'n-stalk, en wid splinters fer a'ms en legs, en a head made out'n elderberry peth, en two little red peppers fer feet.

"Dis yer baby-doll," sez she, "is Hannibal. Dis yer peth head is Hannibal's head, en dese yer pepper feet is Hannibal's feet. You take dis en hide it unner de house, on de sill unner de do', whar Hannibal'll hafter walk ober it ev'y day. En ez long ez Hannibal comes anywhar nigh dis baby-doll, he'll be des lak it is—light-headed en hot-footed; en ef dem two things doan git 'im inter trouble mighty soon, den I'm no cunjuh-'oman. But wen you git Hannibal out'n de house, en git all thoo wid dis baby-doll, you mus' fetch it back ter me, fer it's monst'us powerful goopher, en is liable ter make mo' trouble ef you leabe it lay-in' roun.'"[19]

The Hot Foot Hannibal doll is a spell based on the hoodoo tradition of foot track magic. Foot track magic involves throwing powders and such in the path of a target, who subsequently suffers from abnormal maladies and a run of bad luck. The belief is that the toxic properties of the powder will be absorbed through the foot and infect the individual. Ailments such as back problems, difficulty walking, edema, and difficulty concentrating are some of the complaints of those who have been victimized in this fashion. It is said that the only cure is removal by a root-worker.

Foot track magic occurs in two ways: the direct method, and the sympathetic method. The direct method occurs when a powder or gris gris is thrown on the ground and the person's foot actually touches the substance. The direct method also occurs when a bottle is buried in the path of a target and the individual walks over it. The second method involves capturing the person's footprint by gathering the dirt from an actual footprint of the target, or by taking an old sock or shoe and doctoring it with some other powder or gris gris to jinx or cross the person.[20]

To create the Hot Foot Hannibal conjure doll, make a cloth doll baby and place a hot pepper in each foot. Stuff the arms, legs, and body with corn husks. Stuff the head of the doll baby with dried elderberry pith. The pith of the elder-

---

19. C. W. Chesnutt, "Hot-Foot Hannibal," *Atlantic Monthly* 83: 49-56.
20. D. Alvarado, *The Voodoo Hoodoo Spellbook* (Charleston, SC: Create Space, 2009).

berry bush is the spongy interior part of the stem. Attach a taglock to the doll—a photo, a personal effect, or the person's name written in lead pencil on a piece of torn brown paper (like a grocery bag). Place inside the doll and sew it closed. Put the doll under the front doorstep of the target or bury it in the ground where you know the individual will be walking over it. Leave the doll in place for as long as you want your target to be "light headed and hot footed."

Waxen images used in homeopathic magic.

Mississippi Death Doll

Because this spell belongs in the class of hoodoo spells referred to as *death conjure* or *killing hurts*, it goes without saying that you should not attempt it.[21] It is provided for its folkloric and entertainment value only.

Paper Voodoo doll.

21. Haskins, *Voodoo & Hoodoo*.

If you have an enemy that you want to "disappear," then make this Mississippi paper death doll. When the moon is changing from full to waning, take a newspaper and cut it out in the shape of a person, naming the image after the person you wish to kill. Stick a brass pin in the image multiple times, going from the head to the feet (so as to "bear him down"). Then get a small box and lay the image in it like a man in a coffin. Just as the sun goes down, dig a hole in a cemetery and bury the box. Your enemy will surely die—"goes down wid de sun."[22]

Mississippi Hex Doll

This is another doll baby from the old Mississippi conjure tradition that reportedly makes a person "disappear." Make a doll out of dirt in which earthworms have crawled. You may have to mix it with clay so that it stays together. Use clay from a crawfish hole if you can get it. You will have to moisten the clay, and then allow it to dry. Dress the doll in some of your enemy's dirty clothes. If you cannot get some of their clothes, then wrap the doll in fabric that looks like their clothes. For example, if your enemy wears blue jeans, then get some blue jean fabric and roll it around in the dirt and wrap the doll with it. Name the doll for your enemy.

Actual Mississippi hex doll. Photo by Denise Alvarado.

---

22. N.N. Puckett, *Folk Beliefs of the Southern Negro* (Chapel Hill, NC: The University of North Carolina Press, 1926).

Now this is the tricky part. Place the doll on an ant bed and leave it there for nine days. Be careful with this part because if the ants get on you and bite you, the spell will not work and you will have hexed yourself instead. And well, that would just be unfortunate. On the ninth day, take a shovel and scoop up the doll along with the top part of the ant nest and turn it directly upside down. This must be done on the first attempt. Tap the dirt down thirteen times so that you have firmly planted the doll in the ground. It is said that your enemy will suffer terribly within nine days.

New Orleans Death Rite

The following is a recounting of a severe New Orleans death rite using the coffin described by Zora Neale Hurston in the *Journal of American Folklore*. Its inclusion in this volume is purely for its historical and folkloric value, and serves to illustrate the continuum of spells for which the coffin was utilized in New Orleans.

Make a coffin one-half foot long. Dress a small doll in black and put the doll in the coffin. Write the victim's name on paper and put it in the coffin under the doll. Don't cover the coffin. Dig a trench much longer than the coffin. Take a black cat and put it in the grave. Cover the open grave with cheese-cloth and fix it so the cat can't get out. Take a black chicken and feed it one-half glass of whiskey in which a piece of paper with the victim's name has been soaked. Put the chicken in with the cat and leave them there for a month. They will die. Then put the coffin in and bury it with a white bouquet at the head and foot.[23]

Seven Pins Voodoo

Pins, nails, needles, and fish bones have been used in conjunction with Voodoo dolls, the Nkisi or bocio of Africa, the Greek Kolossoi, and European poppets for centuries. Pins are used to activate the intent of the spell, activate the spirit inside the doll, and attach other items to the doll. The use of pins in seven different colors originated with New Orleans Voodoo, most likely as a result of the tourist trade. The seven pins are often found attached to the mass-produced Voodoo dolls in the French Quarter.

---

23. Haskins, *Voodoo & Hoodoo*.

The simplest way to use pins with a Voodoo doll is to take each pin and concentrate on the color symbolism. Meditate upon how you want these things to manifest in your life. For example, with your yellow pin, focus on what success you desire. After you are very clear about this, stick the pin into your doll in the heart or stomach region. This area will support your heart's desire and your gut feelings or intuition. You can also stick your pins into the head for knowledge. Repeat this process for each pin. A candle may be burned during this process to strengthen your work. Choose a candle color to match your deepest need. The candle colors are the same as the pin colors in this case.

The symbolism of the seven pin colors is as follows:

White: Spiritual cleansing, removing jinxes, protection, blessing, healing, assisting others, reversing hexes, restoring health, all things positive.

Red: Love, passion, romance, energy, lust, fertility, attention, sexuality.

Purple: Power, psychic ability, commanding, compelling, controlling, invocation, peace, protection, abundance.

Green: Money, wealth, prosperity, gambling, luck, fertility, business success.

Black: Removing evil, sending harm, destruction, repelling negativity, protecting, banishing negative people, binding, hexing, jinxing, cursing.

Yellow: Success, mental clarity, communication, fast action, success, and excelling at school or in an academic setting.

Blue: Health, peace, and abundance, sometimes associated with love in New Orleans Voodoo, particularly with works related to Marie Laveaux.

To Make a Person Sickly

This spell is done when you want to make someone ill. Create a cloth doll baby. Attach some horsehair to its head and stuff with Spanish moss, a snake's tooth, and gunpowder. Wrap it in an oil-drenched rag and bury it under your enemy's doorstep or porch.

Tormentor Conjure Doll

This is a Southern hoodoo conjure doll spell typical of those found in the mid-1900s. Make a Voodoo doll out of black fabric and stuff with Spanish moss and a whole can of black pepper. Attach some crow feathers on the head. Write the name of the one to be tormented on a piece of parchment paper with Dragon's Blood ink. Write your curse below the name. Attach the name paper to the doll with a honey locust thorn. Take some Black Arts oil and anoint the feathers with it. Then, anoint the body with Obeah perfume oil. Bury the doll along with a fresh catfish in the backyard of your enemy without their knowledge.

Formula for Obeah Perfume Oil

Use the essential oils or essences for the ingredients listed. The dried herbs can be used in place of oil or as an adjunct to the oil.

Myrrh gum
Patchouli essential oil
Galangal root
Jasmine essential oil
Lemon essential oil

Combine the above ingredients to a base of olive oil to which a small amount of vitamin E has been added as a preservative.

Threefold Payback Wiccan Poppet Spell

Create a poppet out of beeswax using sheets of beeswax that can be purchased from any craft store. Take some personal items of your target, such as hair, nail clippings, a snippet of clothing, or a piece of mail addressed to your target and roll it up in the beeswax. Form a human figure out of the rolled-up beeswax using several pieces if necessary. Cover it with a piece of clothing that belongs to your target. Name the poppet for the person who is the subject of your wrath. The method of torture is now threefold: drive nine nails into the doll, bang it with a hammer, and then burn it. When there is nothing left of the doll, say *"You are nothing. I am free. So be it."*

Demon Doll Spell to Get Even

According to demonologists, the practice of saying the Lord's Prayer backwards is used for casting evil curses. It is said that if one stands before a mirror in a dark room while holding a candle in front of them and reciting the backwards blessing, the devil will come forth.

Build a fire and before it create a Voodoo doll out of wax in the likeness of your enemy. Baptize the doll in the name of your enemy. Repeat the Lord's Prayer backwards nine times while piercing the doll on all sides with pins. When you are done, bury the doll on your enemy's property or someplace over which they will walk. If this is not possible, bury the doll in a cemetery, being sure to leave nine copper pennies when you leave. Do not look back and do not say the name of your enemy again.

The Lord's Prayer Backwards

.nemA .reverof dna won
sruoy era yrolg eht dna ,rewop eht ,modgnik eht roF
.live morf su reviled dna
lairt fo emit eht morf su evaS
.su tsniaga nis ohw esoht evigrof ew sa
snis ruo su evigroF
.daerb yliad ruo yadot su eviG
.nevaeh ni sa htrae no

,enod eb lliw ruoy
,emoc modgnik ruoy
,eman ruoy eb dewollah
,nevaeh ni rehtaF ruO

Hoodoo You Hate Doll

Make a black doll baby. Stuff it with Spanish moss and add some burrs and devil's dung (Asafoetida) and sew closed. Name the doll for your enemy. Sew the mouth with Xs to shut it up and bind its legs with rope, so it cannot go anywhere. Twist its arms and bind to the side of the doll, so it cannot do anything. Light a black candle and continually burn its feet in the flame. Pick up the candle and allow the wax to drip all over the doll. Stick the doll with pins and curse your enemy by name with each stick. Take it somewhere away from your home and place under a large rock to inflict relentless pressure, stress, and headaches on your target. It is ideal if you can place the doll under a large rock on the person's property.

Voodoo Mama's Revenge

Voodoo Mama's revenge is a spell used to seek retribution against someone who has done you a great wrong. Write the name of your oppressor on a black Voodoo doll while burning a black candle. Anoint both doll and candle upside down with Revenge oil. Say Psalm 55 over the doll nine times while the candle burns. When it has burned all the way down, throw the wax remains and the doll against the gate of a cemetery. When you leave, go a different way from whence you came.

Psalm 55: A Prayer for the Destruction of the Deceitful

To the chief Musician on Neg'inoth, Maschil, A Psalm of David
Give ear to my prayer, O God; and hide not thyself from my supplication.
Attend unto me, and hear me: I mourn in my complaint, and make a noise;
Because of the voice of the enemy, because of the oppression of the wicked: for
*   they cast iniquity upon me, and in wrath they hate me.*
My heart is sore pained within me: and the terrors of death are fallen upon me.

Fearfulness and trembling are come upon me, and horror hath overwhelmed me.

And I said, Oh that I had wings like a dove! for then would I fly away, and be at rest.

Lo, then would I wander far off, and remain in the wilderness. Selah.

I would hasten my escape from the windy storm and tempest.

Destroy, O Lord, and divide their tongues: for I have seen violence and strife in the city.

Day and night they go about it upon the walls thereof: mischief also and sorrow are in the midst of it.

Wickedness is in the midst thereof: deceit and guile depart not from her streets.

For it was not an enemy that reproached me; then I could have borne it: neither was it he that hated me that did magnify himself against me; then I would have hid myself from him:

But it was thou, a man mine equal, my guide, and mine acquaintance.

We took sweet counsel together, and walked unto the house of God in company.

Let death seize upon them, and let them go down quick into hell: for wickedness is in their dwellings, and among them.

As for me, I will call upon God; and the LORD shall save me.

Evening, and morning, and at noon, will I pray, and cry aloud: and he shall hear my voice.

He hath delivered my soul in peace from the battle that was against me: for there were many with me.

God shall hear, and afflict them, even he that abideth of old. Selah. Because they have no changes, therefore they fear not God.

He hath put forth his hands against such as be at peace with him: he hath broken his covenant.

The words of his mouth were smoother than butter, but war was in his heart: his words were softer than oil, yet were they drawn swords.

Cast thy burden upon the LORD, and he shall sustain thee: he shall never suffer the righteous to be moved.

But thou, O God, shalt bring them down into the pit of destruction: bloody and deceitful men shall not live out half their days; but I will trust in thee.[24]

Wax Corpse Doll Charm from Malay

Here is a spell from *The Golden Bough* that the author Sir James George Frazer describes as an illustration of homeopathic or imitative magic:

Make a corpse of wax from an empty bees' comb and of the length of a footstep; then pierce the eye of the image, and your enemy is blind; pierce the stomach, and he is sick; pierce the head, and his head aches; pierce the breast, and his breast will suffer. If you would kill him outright, transfix the image from the head downwards; enshroud it as you would a corpse; pray over it as if you were praying over the dead; then bury it in the middle of a path where your victim will be sure to step over it. In order that his blood may not be on your head, you should say:

It is not I who am burying him,
It is Gabriel who is burying him.

Thus, the guilt of the murder will be laid on the shoulders of the archangel Gabriel, who is a great deal better able to bear it than you are.[25]

Witchdoctor's Demon Doll

This is a rather unforgiving spell. It involves evoking a demon, so it should not be attempted by anyone who does not have extensive experience in this area.

Take some softened wax and mold it before a fire into the form of your target, as near as you can represent them. Pierce the image with pins on all sides while reciting the Lord's Prayer backwards. Summon a demon of your choice and offer prayers to the demon that it will fix its stings into the person the wax figure represents. The only way this hex can be countered is for the target to make an

---

24. Scripture quotations taken from the 21st Century King James Version, copyright 1994. Used by permission of Deuel Enterprises, Inc., Gary, SD 57237. All rights reserved.
25. Frazer, *The Golden Bough*.

uncrossing charm and wear it close to the body. The person must repeat the Psalms 109 and 119 every day, or they will remain crossed.

Witch Queen's Revenge Doll

This Voodoo hoodoo curse is based on the legend of the *Louisiana Loup Garou* (pronounced *loo-ga-roo*) and the creation of a vintage-style doll used for sweet revenge, righting wrongs, and getting even. This doll is made with the express purpose of inflicting harm on another individual by making the victim suffer from physical maladies such as a backache, stomach ache, nose bleed, pain of all sorts, and even venereal diseases. In the past, this kind of doll was often referred to as a *Voodoo devil doll,* and its power was considered unparalleled. If you should decide to perform this ritual, use *extreme care* when creating and using the doll.

In Louisiana folklore, the Loup Garou is the werewolf of the bayous, prowling the swamps around Greater New Orleans and Acadiana. There are as many stories of the Loup Garou as there are people telling them. It is said that the Loup Garou has red or yellow-green eyes and huge fangs. Some believe it is an ancestral spirit; others say it is the spirit of a barren woman. Some say it is a person who changes his form with the movement of the moon, either purposefully by using magic, or after being placed under a curse. Most of the time it changes into a werewolf; other times it transforms into a small white animal like a chicken, dog, hog, or squirrel. As a white dog, it is often laden with chains.

On the other hand, the Loup Garou may be a person's double, or a person's soul that leaves the body in a trancelike state to seek out a victim to devour. Or, it may be no more than the animal messenger or familiar of the human being. According to still another version of the lore, it is a man who has sold his soul to the devil. The transformation of the Loup Garou can either be temporary or permanent. In any form, it is a highly feared being that is avoided at all costs.

One local legend in New Orleans tells of a Louisiana bayou woman who was stricken by the curse of the Loup Garou in the 1870s. The famous Marie Laveaux was said to have freed the woman of her curse. According to legend, Mam'zelle Laveaux locked and chained the woman in a cemetery crypt for three nights of the full moon. As many who practice the ancient arts of black magic in Louisiana will tell you, a Loupe Garou can change shape at will. But during the nights and days of the full moon they are trapped in the shape of the creature and are unable to transform at will.[26]

For this ritual, you will call upon the Loup Garou to seek out your enemy. Create this doll during a new moon at midnight in a place lit only by candlelight. Take two pieces of bamboo and tie them together to fashion a cross. Then, wrap the sticks with Spanish moss and cover the moss with black cloth. Tie the cloth in place with a leather cord. Glue a Brazil nut to the top part of the figure with strong craft glue, as this will be the head. Allow it to dry. Stick some black and purple feathers in the top of the head. This doll should be stored in a small coffin or box that functions like a coffin.

Use this doll in a dark, quiet place free from disturbances. Light one black candle and burn some African Ju Ju incense. If you have a cat, keep it in the room with you while you perform this spell.

Call upon the Loup Garou to locate your enemy. Stab the doll where you would like your enemy to experience pain. Do this procedure five nights in a row, just before midnight. On the fifth night, the doll must be destroyed. Do this by smashing its head to bits and throwing the doll into a fire. Gather the ashes and throw them into a river or moving stream.

During the day, keep the doll in the small box or coffin in a dark place. It is believed that if the noonday sun shines on the doll and it casts a shadow, the spell will be broken. [27]

Formula for African Ju Ju Incense

Patchouli leaves
Cedar leaves
Galangal root
Myrrh gum

Grind the above ingredients to a powder using a mortar and pestle and burn on charcoal.

---

26. "Loup Garou American Werewolf Haunted America Tours," http://www.hauntedamericatours.com/vampires/LOUPGAROU/
27. L.F. Snow, "Mail Order Magic: The Commercial Exploitation of Folk Beliefs," *Journal of the Folklore Institute* 16 (1979).

SUPERSTITIONS AND FOLKLORE OF THE SOUTH

In writing, a few years ago, the volume entitled "The Conjure Woman," I suspect that I was more influenced by the literary value of the material than by its sociological bearing, and therefore took, or thought I did, considerable liberty with my subject. Imagination, however, can only act upon data—one must have somewhere in his conciousness the ideas which he puts together to form a connected whole. Creative talent, of whatever grade, is, in the last analysis, only the power of rearrangement—there is nothing new under the sun. I was the more firmly impressed with this thought after I had interviewed half a dozen old women, and a genuine "conjure doctor;" for I discovered that the brilliant touches, due, I had thought, to my own imagination, were after all but dormant ideas, lodged in my childish mind by old Aunt This and old Uncle That, and awaiting only the spur of imagination to bring them again to the surface.

For instance, in the story, "Hot-foot Hannibal," there figures a conjure doll with pepper feet. Those pepper feet I regarded as peculiarly my own, a purely original creation. I heard, only the other day, in North Carolina, of the consternation struck to the heart of a certain dark individual, upon finding upon his doorstep a rabbit's foot—a good omen in itself perhaps—to which a malign influence had been imparted by tying to one end of it, in the form of a cross, two small pods of red pepper!

Most of the delusions connected with this belief in conjuration grow out of mere lack of enlightenment. As primeval men saw a personality behind every natural phenomenon, and found a god or a devil in wind, rain, and hail, in lightning, and in storm, so the untaught man or woman who is assailed by an unusual ache or pain, some strenuous symptom of serious physical disorder, is prompt to accept the suggestion, which tradition approves, that some evil influence is behind his discomfort; and what more natural than to conclude that some rival in business or in love has set this force in motion?

Relics of ancestral barbarism are found among all peoples, but advanced civilization has at least shaken off the more obvious absurdities of superstition. We no longer attribute insanity to demoniac possession, nor suppose that a king's touch can cure scrofula. To many old people in the South, however, any unusual ache or pain is quite as likely to have been caused by some external influence as by natural causes. Tumors, sudden swellings due to inflammatory rheumatism or the bites of insects,

continued

are especially open to suspicion. Paralysis is proof positive of conjuration. If there is any doubt, the "conjure doctor" invariably removes it. The credulity of ignorance is his chief stock in trade—there is no question, when he is summoned, but that the patient has been tricked.

—Charles W. Chesnutt

The Wrath of Jezebel Voodoo Doll Hex

Throughout history, women have carried Jezebel root to render men helpless and subjugate them to their will. Jezebel is the archetypal evil woman identified in the Hebrew Book of Kings as the daughter of Ethbaal, king of the Phoenicians and the wife of Ahab, king of north Israel.[28] The stereotype originates from the passage in 2 Kings 9:30-33 where Jezebel gets killed just after she gets dressed to the hilt.[29]

From a Christian perspective, to be a Jezebel is tantamount to being a promiscuous woman, a pagan, or a traitor masquerading as a servant of God. A Jezebel operates by tricking men and manipulating and/or seducing them into sins of idolatry and sexual immorality, leading them straight to hell.[30] The phrase *painted Jezebel* has entered the mainstream English lexicon, with negative connotations of immorality and prostitution.

This doll spell dispels the stereotype of Jezebel and instead draws upon her strength as a woman and her right to dress as she sees fit. It is designed to empower women who are abused and oppressed. Make this Voodoo doll and perform the following spell during a waning moon. This spell will put a man in his place for treating you badly.

Create a Voodoo poppet out of a Jezebel root (iris hexagona) by stuffing a brown cloth poppet with the root and Spanish moss. Anoint the doll with Jezebel oil, and place in a wide-mouthed mason jar with nine nails and a piece of sulfur. Sprinkle with crossing powder. While you are doing this, you must focus your intention precisely. Talk to the doll as if it were the man who abused you and tell

---

28. 1 Kings 16:31.
29. 2 Kings 9:30-33, New International Version.
30. Revelation 2:20-24, New International Version.

THE VOODOO DOLL SPELLBOOK

him what is going to happen to him. Seal the jar and wrap in a black cloth and secure with a chain. Bury the bottle in the man's yard without letting anyone see you. When you are done, say "Let it be so."

The only way this curse can be lifted is if you dig up the jar yourself and smash it open with a white stone, then burn the contents, scattering the ashes to the east. As you release the ashes, repeat the following:

As the wind scatters these ashes, so shall this curse dissipate. [Name your enemy], *you are released from bondage. It is as it is said.*

Note: In hoodoo, Jezebel root has two primary purposes: for the infamous curse of Jezebel works like the one just described, and to attract a wealthy man. It is used as a lucky amulet by prostitutes to attract high-paying customers and is a main ingredient in the infamous New Orleans Dixie Love formulas.

Gaelic Carp Creaah

This particular spell is said to be found in Northern Scotland among the witchcraft practitioners there. It is designed for times when the witch has extreme hatred for a person, and the work should be done in absolute secrecy. A "body of clay," referred to as "Carp Creaah" in Gaelic, is fashioned to resemble the targeted victim. The Carp Creaah is taken to a running stream out in the wilderness where no one goes and wedged between rocks in the current. This is to keep the doll in place but allow the water to continually run over it. It is said that as the body of clay wastes away from the action of the water, the victim will also waste away and surely die a slow, agonizing death.

The Devil Doll Spell

By Carolina Dean

This is a spell by the wonderfully creative Carolina Dean, who graciously donated a couple of spells for this book. According to Dean, it was designed "on the spur of the moment more than twenty years ago and used in a moment of intense anger." The Devil Doll spell is a fantastic revenge spell that is perfect for anyone consumed by hatred and a deep desire for retribution. The spell "brings out a person's inner demons and drive them down the path of self-destruction," says Dean. "I have only used this spell twice and in each instance achieved results far surpassing my expectations." The following few paragraphs constitute the spell as written by Dean.

The first time I used the spell, I was publicly humiliated by a violent bully and feared for my life. Within twenty-four hours of casting the Devil Doll spell, the bully was stabbed in a bar fight by someone bigger and meaner than he. The bully waited too long to go to the hospital and the wound got infected, which ultimately resulted in a very long recovery during which he lost a great deal of muscle mass and became physically weak. Needless to say, this man was never able to physically intimidate anyone ever again.

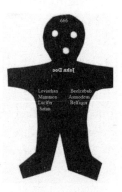

Black cut out doll.

The spell is relatively easy to cast and can be put together with minimal effort. However, it will require the caster to be able to summon a great deal of anger and hatred that is directed at the target through the doll.

To begin, cut a basic human form out of paper and write the name of your target backwards across the chest. Smoke the paper doll in any crossing-type incense and name it after the individual concerned. Next, write the name of those demons associated with the seven deadly sins across the "ribs" of the figure.

Now hold the doll in your hands, and, visualizing their face, think about what the person did to you and how it made you feel. Summon all your anger and hatred for the person and pray:

"Heavenly Father, I beseech you to avenge me of [Name]. *I call on you to set a wicked demon to rule over him and let Satan stand at his right hand and lead him to destruction."*

When your anger is at its peak, violently stab it all over with a needle or pin. As you prick the doll, keep in mind that demons were once believed to enter the body through its orifices or open wounds. Visualize all that anger, hatred, and negative energy entering into the individual as a demonic presence that will ultimately destroy them. Finally, seal your curse by marking the forehead of the doll with the number of the beast and leave the doll where two roads meet.

Disease Doll to Make a Person Sick

This doll baby spell comes from the New Orleans hoodoo tradition. It was reported in Harry Middleton Hyatt's *Hoodoo Conjure Witchcraft Rootwork* as a means of transferring disease from one person to another. It is seemingly very easy to create and deploy.

First, you will have to make a doll baby that you intentionally adorn with bright colors and lots of ribbons. Then, take one of the ribbons and tie a knot in it for each time you have had a particular illness or disease you want to get rid of. Next, take that pretty doll baby and drop it where someone will see it and likely pick it up (I am assuming this is why the doll baby is to be made so pretty). It is said that whoever picks up that doll baby will "catch" the disease or illness, by virtue of the principle of contagious magic, thereby leaving you well.

Original transcription (comment in brackets is Hyatt's):

I make a little doll baby, purty it wid all kids of ribbons, you know, and I can—if I got any kind of disease, just how many times I had it—and I make a knot in there so many times. If I had it three or four times, I makes [three or] *four knots in that piece of ribbon and I tie that doll baby and I go drop it. The one that picks it up is the one that gets that—it be off of me, I won't have it no more. [New Orleans, La., (87 7), 1442:2.]*

Irish Potato Doll to Make a Drunkard

This is another spell from Harry Middleton Hyatt's *Hoodoo Conjure Witchcraft Rootwork*. The original transcription of the interview follows my translation of the spell.

For this spell you need a nice, big Irish potato, a couple of sticks, a couple of pinches of tobacco, some whiskey, and a name paper.

Take the Irish potato and carve a face out of it, leaving enough space to carve a hole in the belly area. The potato represents the victim. Stick two sticks in the potato to represent legs, put some tobacco that has been soaked in whiskey in the hole, and then add a name paper, which is simply a piece of paper with the victim's name written on it. Next, light the tobacco and paper on fire. Burn it until everything in the hole is all burned up. It is said that as it burns, and as the potato shrivels, your victim will be so down in the dumps that they will turn to the bottle for relief.

Original transcription (comments in brackets are Hyatt's):

Take de Irish potato an' make a face outa de Irish potato, de face an' de nose, an' then take a stick an' make de laigs, an' then cut de center out of it—yo' have tub git a nice one. Well, then yo' put tobacco down in there, but yo' soak it in whiskey. An' den yo' burn dat person [name] in dere an' jes' keep 'em drunk all de time. An' jes' as that ole potato shrivel up, they jes' shrivel an' 'kick off from liquor.

(You take that name and write it on a piece of paper and stick in there, and the tobacco is soaked in whiskey. That is to make a person become onry [ornery] or just make them down-and-out).

Yes, down—dey jes' be so low that they wanta drink an' drag an' smoke constantly.[31]

---

31. Hyatt, H.M. (1935) *Hoodoo-Conjuration-Witchcraft-Rootwork* Vol 1. Western Publishing, Inc., Hannibal, Mo.

[Apparently, the potato rite can be used either to cure a person from drinking or make him a drunkard—your intention determining which].

New Orleans Coffin Spell to Kill a Woman

New Orleans is notorious for its many versions of coffin spells. Here is yet another one that is designed to kill a woman. It is from Harry Middleton Hyatt's *Hoodoo Conjure Witchcraft Rootwork*. The original transcription of the interview follows my translation of the spell.

Procure a small doll and name it after the target. Say to the doll, "[Name], I want you to pass out in nine days." Get a box in the shape of a coffin or one that can serve as a coffin. Shroud the doll with some kind of lightweight fabric like muslin or organza, and place the shrouded doll in the coffin. Then, put the doll that is inside the coffin into another box—which serves to disguise what you actually have—and bury the coffin inside the box. Put some sticks in the box to make it look like a fence around the grave.

After nine days, take the whole box up to a cemetery and bury it next to the grave of someone you know, telling them that you are putting this person there to keep them company.

Original transcription (comments in brackets are Hyatt's):

If it's a woman yo' wants tuh kill, yo' take an' git chew a little doll, an' let it be a she doll an' yo' name that doll, lak mah name's Catherine [once before, she called herself Catherine—probably her name], *yo' name dat doll Catherine. An' now yo' say to me, say, "Catherine, ah want chew tuh pass out in nine days." Yo' see. Now, yo' take an' git chew a box dat be shape lak a little coffin. Yo' shroud me an' yo' put me in dere. See, yo' name me—see, yo' got mah name on dere. Yo' put me in dere an' yo' bury it—make a little grave all around dere an' put dat in a box. Yo' understan' whut ah mean? An' den yo' take dat—honey, see lak tomorrow be de nine days, yo' take dat today an' yo' carry it on up to de cemetery. Anybody dat chew know dat passed out, yo' put me in dere wit dem, an' den tell dem dat chew want me tuh keep dem company. Ah don't care if— ah fall down an' break mah neck—somepin goin' happen tuh me. Ah gotta go back dere—when de nine days up dey got company dere.*

(You put this little box right down in that grave. Do you put it any special way in that grave? What do you do with those sticks?)

Yo' see, de sticks is goin' be in dat box [with the doll], *yo' see. Yo' put me in a coffin. Den yo' take an' put me* [in the little coffin] *into a box* [another box], *yo' see, dat chew'll be able tuh carry an' people don't see dat chew got a coffin—it* [the first box with the doll] *de shape of a coffin, yo' understan'. Dey'll think it's a ordinary box or somepin yo' got, an' yo' ain't. An' yore sticks is goin' be aroun' dere* [outside and about the first box] *but into dere* [the second box], *yo' see. Den nobody will see what chew got.*

(What are the sticks in there for—any particular reason?)

Dem sticks is de graveyard—dat's de fence aroun' de grave.

EFFIGY HANGING OF PEDOPHILES

In the 1970s, anthropologists observed a ceremonial reaction to the breaching of incest taboo in the coastal village of Texier on the West Indian island of St. Vincent. Villagers described an activity that they called hangings of those found guilty of incest. These hangings are symbolic trials and executions of effigies created to represent the guilty parties. On a psychological level, the effigy hangings serve as a means for the community to express a collective aversion to incest. On a spiritual and magical level, the effigy hangings are a sympathetic means of punishing offenders.

The effigy hangings of pedophiles and other sexual deviants consist of two different but related activities: a mock jury trial similar to the court proceedings used in the larger society, and a ritual hanging of life-size effigies that represent the guilty parties. Members of the community act as judge, policemen, jury members, bailiffs, prosecuting and defense attorneys, witnesses, defendants, and family members of the defendants. Those in assigned roles are given silly names to provide comic relief to an otherwise distasteful and horrendous situation. Attorneys engage in loud and obnoxious debates, community members interrupt the proceedings with comments and shouting, and witnesses provide personal accounts of the events. After the jury hands down the guilty verdict, the judge proclaims: "The defendants shall be hung by the neck until they are dead. May God have mercy on their souls." He then signs the death decree, at which time the family members of the condemned express their grief by crying and weeping.

Following sentencing, there is a two-week period where the effigies are on public display in a place where nightly dancing takes place. On the first full moon following sentencing, a steel band leads a procession of villagers to the site and plays music throughout the night. The effigies are pulled to the tops of long bamboo poles and paraded in a humorous fashion through the streets until the ropes are suddenly pulled and the necks break. The effigies are then shot with a rifle by a marksman; a public dance follows.[32]

---

32. H. Rubenstein, "Incest, Effigy Hanging, and Biculturation in a West Indian Village," *American Ethnologist* 3 (1976): 765-781.

NAIL FETISHES AMONG THE BANTU & SOUTH AFRICA[33]

Among the Central, South-eastern, and South-western tribes idols are unknown. The objects which have sometimes been described as idols are merely dolls. Most of these dolls are no more than playthings, though some are carried by women as amulets to produce children. A sort of amulet or fetish is made, as already mentioned (p.356), by the Baronga at a chief's death, of portions of his exuviae. Among the Northern tribes idols are of the rarest occurrence. The sacred spear of the Warundi is hardly an idol. The Achewa of North-eastern Rhodesia are said to conjure the spirit of the dead into a doll or image composed of small peces of wood enclosing a tiny box made of the handle of a gourd-coup; the whole is bound round with calico and bark-rope, and afterwards receives the prayers of the survivors. Elsewhere in the neighbour-hood of Lake Tanganyika, the habitation of the disembodied soul is a carved human image. It is set up in or near a village, and prayers and sacrifices are addressed to it (FL xiv. 61). An image of a god is reported on apparently good authority to have existed at Mwaruli, tended by priestesses, who were called the wives of the god. This seems to require further investigation. Among the Western tribes the case is different. As has been already (§ 4) noted, images are used in the worship of the dead, as well as family fetishes comparable with those of the Baronga chiefs. On the West Coast the objects most usually associated in the mind of Europeans with the religion of the natives are called 'fetishes.' Properly speaking, the word fetish (from the Portuguese feitiço) means 'sorcery' or 'amulet.' Fetishes are of two kinds, protective and imprecatory. The protective class consists of wooden human (prequently ithyphallic) figures and objects of various other substances and shapes. Some of them are regarded as personal beings, or at least, as possessed of an indwelling spirit; others are mere amulets. When one of the former is made, a man (or, according to the kind of fetish, a woman) who is a member of the family for which it is made is chosen as its custodian and spokesman. A ceremony of consecration is performed by the nganga, by which the spirit, or voice, is supposed to enter the spokesman's head. The spirits of such fetishes are said to be brought by one or other of the winds. The imprecatory fetishes

---

33. Encyclopaedia of religion and ethics, Volume 2, James Hastings, John Alexander Selbie, Louis Herbert Gray T&T Clark 1910.

consist entirely of wooden figures, generally human, into which nails are driven from time to time, and which are therefore known as nail-fetishes. Into every one of these fetishes the spirit of some known person is conjured when it is made. It is first decided whose spirit is to be secured. The nganga then goes with a party into the bush and calls out the name of the doomed man. Having done that, he proceeds to cut down a tree, from which it is believed that blood gushes forth. A fowl is killed, and its blood is mingled with that of the tree. The fetish is shaped from the tree, and the person named dies, certainly within ten days; his spirit, in fact, is thenceforth united with the fetish. The nail-fetish is used for two purposes. Oaths are sworn by it: the person swearing calls upon it to kill him if he do or have done such and such a thing, and he thereupon drives a nail into it. At a 'big palaver' (dispute or lawsuit) the fetish is brought out, and each of the parties strikes it, thus imprecating death upon himself if he do not speak the truth. The other purpose for which nail-fetishes are used is to call down evil upon another person. The client goes to the fetish, makes his demand, and drives a nail into it. The palaver is then settled, as far as he is concerned. 'The kulu (spirit) of the man whose life was sacrificed upon the cutting of the tree sees to the rest' (Dennett, Black Man's Mind, 85 ff.). Numerous examples of the nail-fetish are to be seen in European museums, of which the finest, perhaps, is one called 'Mavungu,' left by Miss Kingsley to the Pitt-Rivers Museum at Oxford. The nail-fetishes, however, because used for purely imprecatory purposes, are regarded quite differently from all other objects of prayer or supernatural beings. They are connected in the minds of the people with hostile magic rather than with religion. Their priests form a class apart.

FOUR

DREAM DOLLS
OF ANTIQUITY

Doll magick was a hallmark of ancient Egyptian cultural and magickal traditions. Not only have dolls been discovered in tombs and associated with funerary rites, but they were also associated with dream work. For example, there are references in ancient magickal papyrus texts to dream dolls that were created and rituals that were performed to induce prophetic dreams, as well as to send dreams to others. Magickal dolls called *sympathy dolls* were created in the likeness of the dreamer. After analyzing the constellations and adorning the dolls with symbols of the gods, the Egyptians used the sympathy dolls to direct a dreamer to dream about specific topics, reveal information, and gain answers to questions.

Close analysis of the papyri reveals evidence for the use of magickal dream dolls in ancient Egypt. The magickal papyri were only discovered in the 19th century, and the first complete translation was done in 1986. These ancient papyrus texts provide a fascinating glimpse into the syncretic Greco-Egyptian magical and religious systems. Ancient Egyptian gods and goddesses are found alongside Greek deities and Christian angels. Powerful names, seals, symbols, talismans, formulae, magical songs, dolls, and lamps are among the characteristics of this unique brand of magick.

In ancient Egypt, dolls were fashioned out of wood, clay, wax, or stone. A review of the ancient texts, however, suggests that most magickal works utilized dolls made of wax. Dolls that were worn as amulets or talismans were apparently made from wood or stone. According to Budge:

> It has been said above that the name or the emblem or the picture of a god or demon could become an amulet with power to protect him that wore it, and that such power lasted as long as the substance of which it was made lasted, if the name, or emblem, or picture was not erased from it. But the Egyptians went a step further than this, and they believed that it was possible to transmit to the figure of any man, or woman, or animal, or living creature, the soul of the being which it represented, and its qualities and attributes. The statue of a god in a temple contained the spirit of the god which it represented, and from time immemorial the people of Egypt believed that every statue and every figure possessed an indwelling spirit.
>
> And it is stated in all seriousness that if a piece of papyrus upon which a figure of the monster has been drawn, and a wax figure of him be burnt in a fire made of a certain kind of grass, and the prescribed words be recited over them as they burn, the Sun-god will be delivered from Âpep, and that neither rain, nor cloud, nor mist shall be able to prevent his light from falling upon the earth.[34]

Following are spells based on the ancient Egyptian papyrus texts, substituting some of the required items with ingredients that are accessible in today's world. The spells are simplified for practicality.

Magickal Hermes Doll for Dream Prediction

For this spell, you will need to create a doll out of whatever material you want, though I encourage you to use a natural material and clean, white linen. The doll you create will be a crude representation of Hermes. Don't get too hung up on creating a masterpiece unless you are an artist and are so inclined. Otherwise, just do the best you can. Consider the following information given about Hermes to help you with the construction of your doll.

---

34. E.A. Wallis Budge, *Egyptian Magick* (Mineola, NY: Dover, 1901).

Hermes was the great Olympian messenger god and bringer of dreams to mortals. He was also the patron of boundaries, travel, commerce, shepherds, diplomacy, trade, thievery, language, orators, literature and poets, humor and wit, athletics, writing, astronomy, and astrology, and was a guide to the underworld, among other things. He was also the personal agent and messenger of Zeus, the king of the gods. Hermes was depicted as an elderly bearded man or a handsome and athletic young man. His symbols included the tortoise, the cock, the winged sandals, and a wand entwined with two snakes (caduceus). Hermes was considered a trickster god and is likened to the Roman god Mercury and the Voodoo Loa Legba.

Take your doll and consecrate it in the name of Hermes. Write the following incantation with myrrh ink on a piece of parchment paper and anoint with olive oil:

> By the mystery of death and reincarnation, resurrection, and transformation, bathe this doll in light, give him/her new life, and welcome him/her into new life of baptism, give him/her a new name, the divine and magickal name of Hermes.

Slip the paper inside the doll. Set your magickal Hermes doll on a small wooden shrine. In ancient Egypt, the shrine would be fashioned from linden wood. A quick and easy way to make a wooden shrine is to simply take a small drawer and set it on its end. You can then place some of Hermes' favorite things in the shrine, such as small figurines of a turtle and a rooster. You can cut out a picture of a lindenwood tree and glue it to the back of the shrine.

In the evening before you go to sleep and after you have bathed, go to the shrine and light a white candle. Repeat the following seven times:

> SACHMOUNE [i.e., Sakhmet] PAE'MALIGOTE'RE'E'NCH, the One who Shakes, who Thunders, who has Swallowed the Serpent, Surrounds the Moon, and Hour by Hour Raises the Disk of the Sun, CHTHETHO'NI is Your Name. I ask You, Lords of the Gods, SE'TH CHRE'PS: reveal to me concerning the Things I wish.

Write out your question about the future again and set it at the feet of your Hermes doll. Light some temple incense and go to sleep. You should dream the answer you seek.

Formula for Temple Incense

The following formula for temple incense is drawn from the Book of Exodus and the Talmud. There is a Biblical prohibition against replicating the incense for non-Temple use: "Whoever makes it shall be cut off from his kin," (Exodus 30:37); however, the formula below substitutes cloves for tziporen, which is actually the operculum (trap door to the entrance of the shell) of a species of sea snail. The operculum is ground to powder and since ancient times has been used as a fragrance.[35]

Balsam
Clove (tziporen)
Galbanum
Pure frankincense
Myrrh
Cassia
Spikenard
Saffron
Costus
Aromatic bark
Cinnamon

Blend equal amounts in powder form and burn as needed.

Request for a Dream Oracle

Mix up an herbal dream blend of the following magickal herbs: caraway seeds, marjoram leaves, spearmint leaves, basil leaves, hibiscus flowers, calendula, anise seeds, parsley leaves, cumin, licorice roots, and chamomile seeds. Take a piece of clean white linen and write on it the following formula:

HARMIOUTH LAILAM
CHO'OUCH ARSENOPHRE' PHRE'U PHTHA
   HARCHENTECHTHA.

---

35. "Avraham's Temple Oil Research: The Eleventh Ingredient," http://www.avaroma.com/blog/the-eleventh-ingredient/.

Now, make a doll out of the linen and stuff the doll with the herbal dream blend. Lay the doll between two white candles. In the evening when you are about to go to sleep, light the candles and hold the doll while saying the following formula seven times:

SACHMOUNE [i.e., Sakhmet] *PAE'MALIGOTE'RE'E'NCH, the One who Shakes, who Thunders, who has Swallowed the Serpent, Surrounds the Moon, and Hour by Hour Raises the Disk of the Sun, CHTHETHO'NI is Your Name. I ask You, Lords of the Gods, SE'TH CHRE'PS: reveal to me concerning the Things I wish.*[36]

Extinguish the candles, place the doll on the pillow next to you, and go to sleep. If the spirits are pleased, you will have the answers you seek.

Saucer Divination of Aphrodite

For this spell, you will create a doll to represent the Greek goddess of love, Aphrodite. Use pink or red cloth for her body, and stuff her with cinnamon chips crushed well (or you can use powder, but you would have to use a lot more powder than small chips), rose petals, and marjoram. Marjoram was a favorite herb of the Greek goddess. It was said that if a girl put marjoram on her bed, Aphrodite would visit her and reveal her future spouse. Once you create your doll, set her on your altar. Right before bedtime, follow the directions provided below in the Greek Magickal papyri.

Having kept oneself Pure for 7 days, take a White Saucer, fill It with Water and Olive Oil, having previously written on Its Base with Myrrh Ink: "E'IOCH CHIPHA ELAMPSE'R ZE'L A E E' I O Y O'" (25 letters [in Greek]); and beneath the Base, on the outside: "TACHIE'L CNTHONIE' DRAXO'" (18 letters). Wax over with White Wax. On the outside of the Rim at the Top: "IERMI PHILO' 6 ERIKO'MA DERKO' MALO'K GAULE' APHRIE'L I ask" (say it 3 times). Let It rest on the Floor and looking intently

---

36. *The Greek Magical Papyri in Translation, Including the Demotic Spells*, Volume 1, Hans Dieter Betz, Ed. (Chicago: University of Chicago Press).

at It, say "I call upon You, the Mother and Mistress of Nymphs, ILAOCH OBRIE' LOUCH TLOR; Come in, Holy Light, and give Answer, showing Your Lovely Shape!"

Then look intently at the Bowl. When you see Her, welcome Her and say, "Hail, Very Glorious Goddess, ILARA OUCH. And if You give me a Response, extend Your Hand." And when She extends It, expect Answers to your Inquiry.

But if She does not listen, say, "I call upon the ILAOUCH who has begotten Himeros, the Lovely Horai and You Graces; I also call upon the Zeus-sprung Physis [Nature] of All Things, two-formed, indivisible, straight, foam-beautiful Aphrodite. Reveal to me Your Lovely Light and Your Lovely Face, O Mistress ILAOUCH. I conjure You, Giver of Fire, by ELGINAL, and by the Great Names OBRIE'TYCH KERDYNOUCHILE'PSIN NIOU NAUNIN IOUTHOU THRIGX TATIOUTH GERTIATH GERGERIS GERGERIE' THEITHI. I also ask You by the All Wonderful Names, OISIA EI EI AO' E'Y AAO' IO'IAIAIO' SO'THOU BERBROI AKTEROBORE GERIE' IE'OYA; bring me Light and Your Lovely Face and the True Saucer Divination, You shining with Fire, bearing Fire all around, stirring the Land from afar, IO' IO' PHTHAIE' THOUTHOI PHAEPHI. Do it!"

Preparation: having kept yourself Pure, as you learned, take a Bronze Drinking Cup, and write with Myrrh Ink the previously inscribed Stele [charm or amulet] which calls upon Aphrodite, and use the untouched Olive Oil and clean River Water. Put the Drinking Cup on your Knees and speak over it the Stele mentioned above, and the Goddess will appear to you and will reveal concerning what Things you wish.[37]

---

37. The Greek Magical Papyri in Translation, Including the Demotic Spells, Volume 1, Hans Dieter Betz, Ed. (Chicago: University of Chicago Press).

FIVE

BEND-OVER SPELLS

Bend-over spells are in a class of persuasive spells called *commanding*. These spells are designed to manipulate someone to do your bidding. They are used to subjugate the will of any person, such as a partner or employer, so that they will easily and willingly do whatever it is you want them to do.

As a general rule, the best time to do bend-over spells is on Saturday during the full or waxing moon. Occult practitioners agree that working with the moon phases can enhance your work, but whether or not you do so is up to you. The dolls you create for these spells should be made out of brown (for court cases and legal work) or purple cloth, as these colors are often associated with spells of mastery, influence, commanding, compelling, and bending to one's will.

Triple Strength Bend-Over Voodoo Doll Spell

First, create a brown Voodoo doll or poppet. Write the name of the one you choose to have bend to your will nine times on brown paper and attach it to the doll with a pin. Light a brown candle. Anoint the doll daily with three drops of Essence of Bend-Over oil while stating the person's name and exactly what you want them to do. Repeat for nine days in a row. Keep the doll wrapped in purple cloth and store it away in a place where it will not be seen or handled by others. Repeat every full moon for three months to keep the person under your influence.

Formula for Essence of Bend-Over Oil

Use the essential oils or essences for the ingredients listed. The dried herbs can be used in place of oil or as an adjunct to the oil.

> *Frankincense*
> *Honeysuckle*
> *Vetivert*
> *Calamus root essential oil*
> *Licorice root*
> *Bergamot leaf or bergamot essential oil*
> *High John root*

Blend equal amounts of the above ingredients in an almond oil base to which a small amount of vitamin E has been added.

Magnetic Love Doll to Bring Back a Wayward Lover

Make a Voodoo moss doll out of red fabric and insert two highly magnetic lodestones inside the doll. Write the name of the one you desire to return to you nine times on pure parchment paper with Dove's Blood ink. With a red pin, attach the paper to the Voodoo doll in the heart area. Take a red candle and light it, letting the wax drip on the name paper until the wax covers the name of your lover. Place three drops of Commanding oil on the doll daily for nine days, then three drops daily afterwards until your lover returns. Do not stalk, harass, or bother your target love in any way while performing this ritual.

Formula for Commanding Oil

Use the essential oils or essences for the ingredients listed. The dried herbs can be used in place of oil or as an adjunct to the oil.

> *Bergamot essential oil*
> *Bay essential oil*
> *Red clover tops*
> *Balm of Gilead oil*

Blend equal amounts of the above ingredients in a base of almond oil to which a small amount of vitamin E has been added. Add a few red clover tops to the oil.

You may adjust the ingredients to suit your needs.

Change Someone's Mind

Anoint three black candles with Do As I Say oil. Burn them for half an hour and then melt them. Write your target's name on a piece of purple silk, four times backwards and five times forward, and mix into the wax, forming a ball. Take the ball of wax and some licorice root and insert it into a purple doll baby. Throw the doll baby under your target's house or bury in their front yard. Write your target's name once on another piece of purple silk. Take a coconut and drill a hole in it. Place the piece of purple silk in the coconut and cover with honey. Roll the coconut from the front door to the back door of your house while repeating, "Your head is as hard as a coconut but you are going to change your mind." Then state out loud what you want your target to think. Then take the coconut, roll it up to your target's front door, and leave it there.

SIX

SPELLS FOR
LOVE & ROMANCE

Invite romance, encourage reunion, stimulate sexual relations, draw love, and create harmonious relationships with any of the spells included in this section. For best results, perform the following rituals on a Friday under a waxing or full moon.

Bring Your Lover Back Voodoo Doll Spell

Probably the most common type of love spell is the spell that will bring back a lost lover. Take his or her photograph and place it face down on a table. Place a red candle on top of the photo. Burn red candles on it for three hours in the evening and three hours in the morning for six days. Turn the picture face up and continue the candle-burning ritual for three more days. This will bring the person back.

Faithful Muchacho Love Spell

This is a spell from the Mexican brujaria tradition designed to keep a man's eyes from wandering. Procure a doll made from any red material available and name it for your man. Blindfold the doll with a strip of white cloth and light a Seven-Day

Candle for Our Lady of Guadalupe. Every day for seven days, recite the following prayer to Our Lady of Guadalupe:

> *Our Lady of Guadalupe,*
> *I ask for your intercession to help me and to*
> *help all those who invoke you in their necessities,*
> *O Mystical Rose, hear my prayer and my petition, especially for the one I am*
> *   praying for right now as it is most urgent*
> [Now pray that she will make your man see only you and not desire any-
> one else].
> *As you are the Blessed Virgin Mary*
> *and Mother of the true God,*
> *obtain for us from your most holy Son*
> *the grace of keeping our faith,*
> *of sweet hope in the midst of the bitterness of life,*
> *of burning charity, and the precious gift*
> *of final perseverance.*
> *Amen.*

On the seventh day, remove the blindfold from the doll and thank Our Lady of Guadalupe for hearing your request. Keep the doll wrapped in white cloth and safely hidden away in your bedroom.[38]

Greco-Roman Love Spell

Make two waxen figures: one in the form of Ares, and the other in the form of a woman. The female figure should be kneeling with her hands tied behind her, and the male figure should stand over her with his sword at her throat. Write a large number of the names of demons on the limbs of the female figure. When this has been done, the lover must take thirteen bronze needles and stick them in her limbs, saying as he does so, "I pierce [the name of the limb] that she may think of me." The lover must next write certain words of power on a leaden plate, which must be tied to the wax figures with a string containing 365 knots, and both figure and plate are

---

38. Adapted from M. Devine, *Magic from Mexico* (St. Paul, MN: Llewellyn, 1990).

to be buried in the grave of someone who has died young or has been slain by violence. The lover must then recite a long incantation to the infernal gods. If all these things are done in a proper manner, the lover will obtain the woman's affections.[39]

Gris Gris Doll for a Successful Marriage

This Voodoo doll spell comes straight out of the New Orleans Voodoo hoodoo tradition. In New Orleans, gris gris (pronounced *gree gree*) comes in several forms. It can be a bag filled with items for a particular magickal purpose, or it can be a doll created for a particular magickal purpose. The gris gris is the magick, it is the act of creating the charm, and it is the resulting bag or doll as well. I explain it further in my book *Voodoo Dolls in Magick and Ritual*:

> *In New Orleans, which can be considered the contemporary hub of Voodoo dolls in America, they* [dolls] *are created as gris gris (pronounced* gree gree)*, a form of talismanic magick. The word* gris *means* grey, *denoting that which lies between black and white. Gris gris is both a noun and a verb, referring to a ritually prepared object such as a doll or a small cloth bag filled with magickal ingredients, as well as the act of working the gris gris (i.e. spell or charm).*[40]

The term *gris gris* comes from the Mande language found in the region of Senegal and Mali. In Louisiana, it was integrated into the Voodoo lexicon as a result of the transatlantic slave trade.

This spell is an interesting and excellent example of the blend of Catholicism and hoodoo found in New Orleans-style Voodoo. For this spell, you will need to gather the following items:

2 red doll babies
Rose petals
Red clover
Red ribbon
Sugar

---

39. "Egyptian Magic," http://www.eso-garden.com/specials/egyptian_magic.pdf.
40. D. Alvarado, *Voodoo Dolls in Magic and Ritual* (Charleston, SC: Create Space, 2009).

9 red candles
Champagne
Parsley
Macaroni

Create two doll babies out of red fabric and stuff with rose petals, red clover, and Spanish moss. Attach a taglock to each doll. Tie the two dolls' hands together with a red ribbon. Next, make a mound out of the sugar, place the dolls on top of the mound, and stick the nine red candles into the sugar around the dolls. Sprinkle champagne over the mound and petition St. Joseph by saying the following:

Saint Joseph, make this marriage and I'll pay.

Once the marriage has taken place, put a plate of macaroni sprinkled with parsley near a tree in Congo Square in payment.[41] Pray Psalm 67 daily for added strength.

Psalm 67

God be merciful unto us, and bless us; and cause his face to shine upon us; Selah.
That thy way may be known upon earth, thy saving health among all nations.
Let the people praise thee, O God; let all the people praise thee.
O let the nations be glad and sing for joy: for thou shalt judge the people
*   righteously, and govern the nations upon earth. Selah.*
Let the people praise thee, O God; let all the people praise thee.
Then shall the earth yield her increase; and God, even our own God, shall
*   bless us.*
God shall bless us; and all the ends of the earth shall fear him.[42]

Keep Your Man Faithful

While you man is asleep, cut off a bit of your hair. Procure some of his pubic hair and semen. Take the hair, pubic hair, semen, and some magnolia leaves and flowers

---

41. There are several versions of this spell. I remember being told this version as a child. The basic version of this spell can be found in Saxon, Dreyer, and Tallant, *Gumbo Ya Ya Folk Tales of Louisiana* (Gretna, LA: Pelican Publishing Company, 1988).

42. Scripture quotations taken from the 21st Century King James Version, copyright 1994. Used by permission of Deuel Enterprises, Inc., Gary, SD 57237. All rights reserved.

and put them in a small cloth doll. Tie three knots on the end of a string and say a "Hail Mary" as you tie each knot. Coat the string with a bit of semen. Wrap the doll tightly three times with the string. Put the doll under the front steps and it is said your man will remain faithful.

Hail Mary

Hail Mary, full of grace.
Our Lord is with thee.
Blessed art thou among women,
and blessed is the fruit of thy womb,
Jesus.
Holy Mary, Mother of God,
pray for us sinners,
now and at the hour of our death.
Amen.

Love Doll Spell

Make a doll out of cinnamon dough (see *Spice Up Your Sex Life Love Doll Spell* later in this chapter). When the doll has dried, take a red candle and singe the bottom of its feet while saying:

You burn for me as I yearn for you.

Be careful not to burn the feet too badly. Before you know it, your lover should come running straight to you. When you are not working with your doll, keep it wrapped in a clean white cloth, away from nosy neighbors, prying eyes, and hungry critters.

Love Me Voodoo Doll Spell

Create a doll out of red silk fabric. Cut out two pieces of fabric in the shape of a man or a woman and stitch together, leaving a small opening. Fill with red clover and rose hips and sew up the hole. During the new moon, attach a photo of your beloved and a photo of yourself on top of each other to the doll with a red pin. As you do so, repeat the following over and over:

Face to face, heart to heart,
You and I will never part.

Wrap the doll in red tulle, such as that used on wedding gowns, and keep in your pillowcase.

Love Talisman Spell

Draw a love talisman and write your full name on the back of it. Then, write your lover's name on top of your name. Fold the petition twice, each time folding the paper towards you. Pin the petition to the doll in the heart area with the red pin while saying:

Face to face and heart to heart
You and I will never part.
Your love is mine
My love is yours
So mote it be.

Every day for three days, hold your doll close to your heart and repeat the chant while visualizing you and your lover together. On the third day, burn the petition in the flame of a red candle and scatter the ashes in the direction of your lover. Wrap your Voodoo doll along with the talisman in a red cloth and keep somewhere safe in your bedroom.

Make Me Irresistible Voodoo Doll Spell

Make a pink poppet and stuff with lavender, rose petals, cinnamon, French Love powder, and red clover. Attach a St. Valentine medal to the doll and anoint daily with Fire of Passion oil.

Formula for Fire of Passion Oil

Use the essential oils or essences for the ingredients listed. The dried herbs can be used in place of oil or as an adjunct to the oil.

Saffron
Damiana
Rose
Cinnamon
Musk
Patchouli leaves

Add equal amounts of the above ingredients to a one-ounce base of sweet almond oil to which a small amount of vitamin E has been added. Add a pinch of patchouli leaves to the bottle.

The above formula and its proportions are just one formula; you may adjust ingredients to suit your needs.

Muchachita (Little Girl) Sweetener Spell

There is a category of love spells referred to as sweetener spells. These spells typically employ the use of honey or sugar and are designed to cool down or sweeten up an angry loved one, make a nagging lover whisper sweet nothings, or draw someone close to you. This particular sweetener spell comes from the Mexican brujeria tradition and is a popular type of spell used by husbands who have angry and discontented wives. You will need a pink doll, a red candle, a dish of whiter sugar, and some honey. Take the doll to be blessed by a bruja, or alternately, bless it yourself by sprinkling it with holy water you have obtained from a church. Set the doll in the dish of white sugar and place the red candle in the dish next to the doll. The pile of sugar should be sufficient to hold the candle upright with ease. Light the candle and think about your wife as a sweet, pleasant person who doesn't have an angry bone in her body. Allow the candle to burn all the way down; when it has burned down completely, drizzle some honey all over the doll and the wax remains as if to glue it all together. Bury everything in a garden of flowers as close to your home as possible. Your wife's attitude should change to a pleasant one very soon.[43]

Pierced Heart Love Spell

Procure some polymer clay and add a few drops of red food coloring to it. Add some personal effects belonging to your target to the clay, such as fingernail clippings, pubic hair, semen, or a lock of hair. Then add some personal effects of yours. The more effects you add, the stronger your spell will be. Mix everything up real good. While you are working the clay, focus your thoughts on working your lover and repeat over and over again:

> *As I work this clay, so I work* [name]. *As I mold you, so shall you do my bidding.*

Bake the clay according to the manufacturer's instructions. On the first day of the new moon, name the doll after your lover by saying the name aloud and scratching or writing the name onto the doll. If you are writing the name, use red ink mixed with a drop of your blood.

Using a thorn from a rose bush, gently prick the doll's heart. Don't prick it too hard or you may give your lover a heart attack! As you prick the doll say:

As this thorn pierces your heart, so let it be pierced with love for me.

Wrap the doll in a clean white cloth and keep it under your mattress until your lover comes to you.

Seven Pins Love Spell

Try this spell to get your lover's attention. First, gather the following ingredients:

> *Red figural candle (this is your doll)*
> *7 pins*
> *7 pink candles*
> *Attraction oil*

---

43. Adapted from M. Devine, *Magic from Mexico*.

French Love powder
Parchment paper
Dove's Blood ink

Conduct this spell on a Friday night during a waxing moon. Draw a circle with the French Love powder and place the seven candles inside the circle in a semicircle shape. Leave an opening in the front to lay the figural candle down. Going clockwise, anoint the first pink candle with the Attraction oil and light it, all the while focusing intently on the one you desire. Go around and light each of the candles in a similar fashion. Take your time and create a clear vision in your mind of how you see yourself with this person. Now, anoint the red figural candle, and gently caress the doll as if it were your lover. Lay the doll in the center of the candles. Write your lover's name on the parchment paper with Dove's Blood ink. Hold one of the pins in the candle flame and say:

As the flame heats up this pin, so shall my lover's desire heat up for me.

Take the first pin and pierce it through the paper into the doll in the heart region. Say:

As I drive this pin into you so shall you be driven to me.

Repeat the invocation six more times, each time heating the pin in the flame and repeating the words given. Once all seven pins have been driven into the doll's heart, sprinkle the doll with the French Love powder and allow the candles to burn all the way down. Once they have done so, wrap the doll in red velvet and keep under your bed. Dispose of the wax remains in a moving river.

Formula for Attraction Oil

Use the essential oils or essences for the ingredients listed. The dried herbs can be used in place of oil or as an adjunct to the oil.

Frankincense
Sandalwood

Myrrh
Cinnamon
Orris root

Add equal parts of the above ingredients to a base of almond oil to which a small amount of vitamin E has been added as a preservative.

Unite Two Lovers

To unite two people in love, create two figures from wax and baptize each in the name of the lovers. Place them face to face and stick three long pins with red tips through the hearts so as to pin them together. Give the images to the one who desires such a union so that she or he might press the wax figures to her or his heart while focusing on the desired relationship.

Spice Up Your Sex Life Love Doll Spell

One of the best known ways to spice up your sex life is by bewitching your target through a doll that represents him or her. This spell requires that you make the doll yourself with cinnamon dough. Spicy, sweet, fun, and a recipe for success, this is one powerful love spell.

How to Make Cinnamon Dough

1½ cups ground cinnamon
1 cup applesauce
1 tablespoon of honey
¼ cup white school glue (like Elmer's)
Bowl
Plastic food wrap
Rolling pin
Wax paper

Cookie cutter in the shape of a figure
Red ribbon or yarn for hanging

Mix cinnamon, applesauce, honey, and glue together in a bowl. The dough should be as thick as cookie dough. Add a bit of water if the dough is too stiff.

Remove from bowl and knead. Put it back in the bowl, cover with plastic wrap, and let sit for at least a half hour.

Remove the dough, knead again to make sure it's smooth. Flatten/roll the dough between waxed paper until it's between one-quarter-inch thick and one-eighth-inch thick.

Cut out a figure using a cookie cutter. Gently place the shape on a piece of clean wax paper. It will take three to five days to dry, and you will need to turn it over a couple of times a day for it to dry evenly and flat.

Don't be surprised to see the doll get smaller during the drying process. Keep this in mind when you pick out the cookie cutter for your figure shape. You will also notice that if you do not turn the ornaments over often enough while they are drying, the edges of the ornaments will curl.

Once your doll has dried, eat a piece of it every evening starting at a new moon, saying, "As you become part of me, so let me become part of you." Do this for nine minutes each day until the moon is full. Repeat at the next new moon and at each new moon until you see the desired results.

St. Joseph Wedding Dolls

St. Joseph is a very popular saint in New Orleans, having been imported to the city by the Sicilians. Ever since, he has been celebrated each year on St. Joseph's Day, when lavish altars are created by the local Catholic Churches as well as in individual homes. Although St. Joseph is known as the patron saint to realtors and the one to go to when a house needs selling, he is also considered the patron saint of families.

This spell draws on the patronage of St. Joseph to influence a man to marry a woman; however, it can be adapted for same-sex couples as well. This is a seven-day spell, so be sure to set it up somewhere out of the sight and reach of others.

Buy a couple of wedding dolls from your local department store—the kind that can be found in the wedding supplies section. The small cake topper size is ideal. Buy a package of gold wedding bands and take out two. You will also need a small statue of St. Joseph, or at least have his picture handy.

Buy or make a small white cake that represents the wedding to be and place the bride and groom on top of the cake. Set St. Joseph in front of the cake, and on either side of him light a white seven-day glass-encased candle. Get a Bible. Open it, set it right in front of St. Joseph, and leave it open. Place the two wedding bands on the open pages.

Say the following prayer to St. Joseph for special favors:

Blessed St. Joseph, tender-hearted father, faithful guardian of Jesus, chaste spouse of the Mother of God, I pray and beseech you, to offer to God the Father, His divine Son, bathed in blood on the Cross for sinners, and through the thrice holy Name of Jesus obtain for us of the eternal Father the favor we implore. Amen.

Now, talk to St. Joseph and tell him what you need. Tell him you are burning these candles for him so that he will help you. Tell him they will burn for seven days, and if he helps you get married, you will praise his name publicly, and tell the world what a wonderful and loving saint he is. Most saints love to be acknowledged publicly, and St. Joseph is no exception.

After all this is done, take the two gold wedding bands and interlock them. These rings are made so that they can be opened, and it is very easy to hook them together.

SEVEN

BINDING SPELLS

A form of magic for which the Voodoo doll is particularly suited is the traditional magick binding spell. In this manipulative form of magick, the practitioner ritually binds the Voodoo doll, charges and names it for the individual in question, and prevents that person from doing harm or evil towards others. The individual who is bound in this way will be unable to set in motion any ill intent, and will be left feeling confused, frustrated, and powerless.

Binding spells are also used in love magick. For these types of spells, the practitioner will bind a lover so that they can be with no one else other than the one they are bound to. In ancient times, bindings were often employed to stop a person from gossiping. They were also used to prevent evil spirits from harming anyone. The available archeological evidence shows that magickal dolls were used in cursing and binding rituals in ancient Greece.[44] These dolls, called Kolossoi, were often paired with curse tablets. The curse tablets were binding spells, a type of curse practiced by the Graeco-Romans that involved invoking the gods to intervene and cause harm to others. The dolls found alongside the curse tablets were crudely fashioned in the likeness of the target and often had their hands and feet bound. Sometimes they

---

44. Faraone, "The Agonistic Context of Early Greek Binding Spells," 3-32.

were pieced with nails. The texts on the curse tablets were etched in tiny letters on thin sheets of lead. They have been found rolled or folded, sometimes around hair or some other personal effect of their target, or pierced with nails. Archaelogists have uncovered some Kolossoi with a blank space in the place where identifying tags would normally be found. There, Kolossoi were presumably prepared that way for purchase by customers. Usually, the tablets and dolls were buried in graves or tombs, thrown into wells or pools, placed in the home of the target, impounded in underground sanctuaries, or nailed to the walls of temples.[45] The evidence suggests that these dolls and tablets were used for many reasons, just as Voodoo dolls are used today.

Binding Your Love

Light a purple candle. Write the name of the one you choose to be irresistible to on white paper. Place the name paper under a red Voodoo doll or poppet and wrap the name paper tightly to the doll with a rope. Wrap your doll in a clean white cloth and place it under your mattress.

Mirror Box to Bind an Enemy

This is a spell for when you feel you have been attacked spiritually and you are in need of some serious spiritual defense. To be successful with this work, you need to find your center so that you operate from that place in your gut that is your rock, confidence, and knowing. Once you find that place, do a thorough cleansing of your home. Sweep your floors clean and put everything in a paper bag. Wash your floors with a spiritual floor wash like Chinese wash or Essence of Van Van and take some Holy oil and anoint all of the doorways and windows in your home. Light a white seven-day candle that you have anointed with the Holy oil and fixed with hyssop herbs. Then burn some camphor or sage to fumigate and purify your newly cleansed home. Hang a mirror at the front door facing outwards. At this time you should be praying Psalm 23 for protection. Next, take an uncrossing bath for thirteen days in a row.

---

45. Roger Tomlin, *Tabellae Sulis: Roman Inscribed Tablets of Tin and Lead from the Sacred Spring at Bath* (1988).

To send everything back to your enemy, you will need to create a mirror box during a waning moon. Get a box to be used just for this purpose, and get some mirrors to line each side of the box on the inside (not the outside). You should have six mirrors, including one for the inside of the top lid. Burn a black candle that has been fixed with Cast Off Evil oil and dusted with uncrossing powder while doing this work. Inside the box you should place a doll that you have made to represent this person. Baptize the doll in your enemy's name.

Place the doll in the mirror-lined box and write a petition paper stating what it is that you want. Be very specific. Add something that belongs to your enemy, such as a photo or date of birth, and attach it to the doll in the box. Surround the doll with peppers and sprinkle with sulphur and goofer dust or revenge powder. As you are sprinkling the powder, say something to this effect: "I bind you [state your enemy's name] from hurting me and my family from this point forward forever and for always. May every evil thing you have ever done be returned to you threefold, may every unkind word you have spoken about me be repeated to you by another, may all of your evil thoughts be bound up in your head to be heard by you and only you as incessant, nonstop chatter. May you remain in this state until such time that you see the error of your ways and willingly and sincerely change into a kind and loving person to all. Until this time, I remand you to bondage of your own making." Then put the lid on the box and tie it real good to symbolically bind the person from hurting you and your family any further.

Take the box to a cemetery and bury it. Ask the spirits of the cemetery to hold your enemy down until your enemy sincerely reforms himself or herself. At the cemetary gate, pay the guardian of the cemetery nine copper pennies, a cigar, and small bottle of rum. When you leave, go a different way than when you came.

When you get home, take a bath of hyssop and rue to cleanse yourself. Dress in white and sleep in white sheets that evening. This applies to anyone who participates in the ritual with you. The work is now done.

Tie an Enemy Up

Light a purple candle and make a purple doll baby. Attach a photo of your enemy or a piece of parchment paper with their name written on it with Dragon's Blood ink. Anoint the doll baby's feet with Hot Foot oil to drive your enemy away. Take a rope and tie the doll's hands behind its back and stick the doll in a corner facing the wall. Every day for nine days, say Psalm 94.

Psalm 94

O Lord God, to whom vengeance belongeth; O God, to whom vengeance belongeth, shew thyself.

Lift up thyself, thou judge of the earth: render a reward to the proud.

LORD, how long shall the wicked, how long shall the wicked triumph?

How long shall they utter and speak hard things? and all the workers of iniquity boast themselves?

They break in pieces thy people, O LORD, and afflict thine heritage.

They slay the widow and the stranger, and murder the fatherless.

Yet they say, The LORD shall not see, neither shall the God of Jacob regard it.

Understand, ye brutish among the people: and ye fools, when will ye be wise?

He that planted the ear, shall he not hear? he that formed the eye, shall he not see?

He that chastiseth the heathen, shall not he correct? he that teacheth man knowledge, shall not he know?

The LORD knoweth the thoughts of man, that they are vanity.

Blessed is the man whom thou chastenest, O LORD, and teachest him out of thy law;

That thou mayest give him rest from the days of adversity, until the pit be digged for the wicked.

For the LORD will not cast off his people, neither will he forsake his inheritance.

But judgment shall return unto righteousness: and all the upright in heart shall follow it.

Who will rise up for me against the evildoers? or who will stand up for me against the workers of iniquity?

Unless the LORD had been my help, my soul had almost dwelt in silence.

When I said, My foot slippeth; thy mercy, O LORD, held me up.

In the multitude of my thoughts within me thy comforts delight my soul.

Shall the throne of iniquity have fellowship with thee, which frameth mischief by a law?

They gather themselves together against the soul of the righteous, and condemn the innocent blood.

But the LORD is my defense; and my God is the rock of my refuge.

And he shall bring upon them their own iniquity, and shall cut them off in their own wickedness; yea, the LORD our God shall cut them off.[46]

After saying the Psalm 94, say the Lord's Prayer three times. Repeat this work three days in a row, keeping the doll in the corner. On the third day when you are finished with your prayers, allow the candle to burn all the way down. Bury the doll along with the wax candle remains under an oak tree and sprinkle with blessed salt. Your enemy will be rendered harmless.

Formula for Hot Foot Oil

Use the essential oils or essences for the ingredients listed. The dried herbs can be used in place of oil or as an adjunct to the oil.

Cayenne pepper
Black pepper essential oil
Chili powder
Sulphur
Oil of cinnamon

Add the above ingredients to a base of mineral oil. Be careful not to get it on your skin as it will undoubtedly cause some irritation.

---

46. Scripture quotations taken from the 21st Century King James Version, copyright 1994. Used by permission of Deuel Enterprises, Inc., Gary, SD 57237. All rights reserved.

BREAK UP SPELLS

Home-breaking rituals are common in hoodoo, though they should not be employed lightly. When you break up a couple who have children, you will be affecting the lives of the children forever. The spirits do not take kindly to people who bring harm to children, so think very carefully before attempting any of these spells.

There are times when breaking up a couple is justified. For example, if there is abuse going on, then someone should intervene. If you are driven to magick in an effort to deal with this type of situation, you should also seek assistance from a domestic violence shelter, crisis center, and law enforcement.

Break Up spells are in the category of *enemy works*. Whenever you perform such work, you should always take a purification bath afterwards to protect you from any negative consequences of your actions. To do this, take an herbal bath containing a handful each of hyssop and blessed salt. Light two white candles and place them at either end of the tub so that when you stand up, you are standing between them. Pour the water over your head seven times while reciting Psalm 51.

Psalm 51

*Have mercy upon me, O God, according to thy lovingkindness: according unto
the multitude of thy tender mercies blot out my transgressions.*

Wash me throughly from mine iniquity, and cleanse me from my sin.

For I acknowledge my transgressions: and my sin is ever before me.

*Against thee, thee only, have I sinned, and done this evil in thy sight: that thou
mightest be justified when thou speakest, and be clear when thou judgest.*

Behold, I was shapen in iniquity; and in sin did my mother conceive me.

*Behold, thou desirest truth in the inward parts: and in the hidden part thou
shalt make me to know wisdom.*

*Purge me with hyssop, and I shall be clean: wash me, and I shall be whiter
than snow.*

*Make me to hear joy and gladness; that the bones which thou hast broken may
rejoice.*

Hide thy face from my sins, and blot out all mine iniquities.

Create in me a clean heart, O God; and renew a right spirit within me.

Cast me not away from thy presence; and take not thy holy spirit from me.

Restore unto me the joy of thy salvation; and uphold me with thy free spirit.

*Then will I teach transgressors thy ways; and sinners shall be converted
unto thee.*

*Deliver me from bloodguiltiness, O God, thou God of my salvation: and my
tongue shall sing aloud of thy righteousness.*

O Lord, open thou my lips; and my mouth shall shew forth thy praise.

*For thou desirest not sacrifice; else would I give it: thou delightest not in burnt
offering.*

*The sacrifices of God are a broken spirit: a broken and a contrite heart, O God,
thou wilt not despise.*

Do good in thy good pleasure unto Zion: build thou the walls of Jerusalem.

*Then shalt thou be pleased with the sacrifices of righteousness, with burnt of-
fering and whole burnt offering: then shall they offer bullocks upon thine
altar.*[47]

---

47. Scripture quotations taken from the 21st Century King James Version, copyright 1994. Used by
permission of Deuel Enterprises, Inc., Gary, SD 57237. All rights reserved.

The Voodoo Doll Spellbook

Break Up a Couple Voodoo Doll Spell

Burn a black candle while you write the names of the ones you choose to break up nine times on brown paper. Write the words "BREAK UP" between their names. Write the name of the person you want in black ink and the person you want to go away in red ink. Place the paper under a black Voodoo doll made from tattered and torn fabric that you have fixed (anointed) with Break Up oil. Place it near the doorstep of your rival. If this is not possible, tie it up real good in black fabric and bury in a cemetery or leave it at a crossroads.

Formula for Break Up Oil

Use the essential oils or essences for the ingredients listed. The dried herbs can be used in place of oil or as an adjunct to the oil.

> *Lemon verbena*
> *Guinea peppers*
> *Cayenne pepper*
> *Powdered sulphur*

Mix the above ingredients in a base of mineral oil.

Home Breaker Ritual

This ritual targets the individual you would like to leave. Make a black conjure doll and secure your target's foot tracks by scooping up some of the dirt and grass where you know they have walked. Place the tracks inside the doll along with some Spanish moss, hair from a black dog, hair from a black cat, sulphur, and Separation powder. Sew the doll shut, and sprinkle with War Water and more Separation powder. Take the doll to a running stream at midnight and say the following:

> *Moss choke it, sulphur smoke it*
> *Fight like cats and dogs and run away.*

Turn around as though ready to leave and throw the doll over your right shoulder into the running water. Leave the area and do not look back or return to that area.

Formula for Separation Powder

Chili powder
Cinnamon
Galangal
Black pepper
Vetivert

Grind the ingredients to a powder with a mortar and pestle and blend well.

Formula for War Water

As with all of the formulas provided in this book, multiple variations are available. The formulas vary according to region, tradition, and preference of the practitioner. Here is an old, traditional formula for War Water that has its origin in New Orleans hoodoo.

Oil of tar
Rusty nails
Swamp water

Combine all of the above ingredients in a wide-mouth mason jar and shake up the mixture. Let it sit for a couple of weeks, periodically opening the jar to encourage oxidation and further rusting of the nails in the water. After a period of time, the water will get rustier and blacker, making it all the more potent.

Separation Spell

This spell is designed to break up a couple by causing them to quarrel. Make two black doll babies and fill each one with the tracks of one person. Add dirt from the grave of a divorced person, hair from a black cat and a black dog, Spanish moss, and pigeon excrement. Place both dolls in a brown paper bag and sprinkle Separation powder into the bag. Shake the bag up real good so that the powder is completely covering the dolls. Tie the bag closed with red string and hang from a tree for three days. On the third evening, take the bag and burn it in a fire at midnight. The spell is complete when the bag and the dolls are completely turned into ash.

Doll Baby to Make a Couple Fight

This is a spell from Harry Middleton Hyatt's *Hoodoo Conjure Witchcraft Rootwork*. To make a couple quarrel with the intention of breaking them up, make a doll baby from a striped pillowcase and stuff it with sawdust, alum, garlic, and bluestone. Be sure to cut the material so that stripes are lengthwise from head to foot. Sew everything up in the doll and place the doll under a mattress, making sure the doll lies with its feet to the east and head to the west. As long as the doll lies undisturbed in that position, the couple will have no rest for quarreling.

Original transcription (comments in brackets are Hyatt's):

You takes ordinary sawdust—just take ordinary sawdust. If you want to make a woman disagreeable—things disagreeable in a home for a woman and her husband, take ordinary sawdust, a piece of garlic, a piece of alum and a piece of bluestone, and powder that. And mix it in that sawdust and sew it up in that form of a person—see, like—just like a little small doll baby—a small piece of it.

[What kind of material would you use for that]

For wrapping that in?

[Yes.]

Bed ticking.

[Any kind?]

No, not any kind, bed ticking—something that a mattress or pillow is made out of, not any kind of material.

[Oh, I see. Well, why is that?]

*Because you wants to lay the stripes according to the rise and fall of the . . .
That's why we do that. You want to make the stripes so that on the shape of
that thing like a person it lays with the rise and fall of the sun. You lays it like
you take a dead person is buried with their head to the east—I mean to the
west and their feet to the east. You lay that thing with the head to the east and
the feet to the west. That's against the life of any person it's under.*

[Now, where do you put this little doll?]

*You put it in—you put it under or in a mattress. But the best way you do, if
you can open the mattress and put it in there, sew it in the mattress. Just know
how you got it—lay it in the position and lay it right in that mattress where
they lay on that. And that woman'll have trouble in her house with her husband as long as she sleeps on it.*[48]

---

48. Hyatt, H. M. Hoodoo *Conjuration-Witchcraft-Rootwork.*

MONEY SPELLS

Easy Money Doll Baby Spell

If you want to get easy money, it is believed that burning onion peels will do the trick. Make a Voodoo poppet out of green material and stuff it with onion peels. Anoint with Fast Luck oil and burn the doll in a cast iron pot until it is nothing but ashes. Take the ashes and put them in a red flannel mojo bag along with a whole nutmeg and silver dime. Carry the bag with you until you get your money.

Hold On to Your Money Voodoo Doll Spell

This Voodoo doll spell is designed to keep your money from burning a hole in your pocket. Make a Voodoo moss doll and stick some sprigs of thyme in the moss. Wrap with blue fabric. Pray Psalm 113 for nine days in a row and repeat monthly as long as spending money is an issue for you. Display the doll prominently in your home where it will be a constant reminder to you to change your spending habits. You can use the same doll to repeat the spell until your behavior is changed.

Psalm 113

Praise ye the LORD. Praise, O ye servants of the LORD, praise the name of the LORD.

Blessed be the name of the LORD from this time forth and for evermore.

From the rising of the sun unto the going down of the same the LORD's name is to be praised.

The LORD is high above all nations, and his glory above the heavens.

Who is like unto the LORD our God, who dwelleth on high,

Who humbleth himself to behold the things that are in heaven, and in the earth!

He raiseth up the poor out of the dust, and lifteth the needy out of the dunghill;

That he may set him with princes, even with the princes of his people.

He maketh the barren woman to keep house, and to be a joyful mother of children. Praise ye the LORD.[49]

Wealth and Prosperity Voodoo Doll Spell

This ritual is to be performed for seven days. It is designed to draw wealth and prosperity to you.

On the morning of a new moon, fix yourself a cup of Money tea made from a teaspoon of loose mint leaves and a teaspoon of loose chamomile leaves. Steep the herbs in hot water for five minutes and sweeten with honey. As you sip the tea, make a Voodoo doll out of fabric that has dollar bills printed on it. If you can't find fabric with money printed on it, just use green or gold fabric. As you sip your tea and create your Voodoo doll, you should be thinking of creating the wealth and abundance you need. Think of nothing else but prosperity. Attach a couple of gold bells to the doll.

Take a piece of virgin parchment paper and write power words and draw talismans that represent your needs and wants. For example, if it is money you want, write "wealth," "prosperity," and so on. Place this paper underneath a seven-day prosperity candle and light some money incense. Take the doll in your hands and

---

49. Scripture quotations taken from the 21st Century King James Version, copyright 1994. Used by permission of Deuel Enterprises, Inc., Gary, SD 57237. All rights reserved.

THE VOODOO DOLL SPELLBOOK

begin to gently shake it so as to ring the bells. While shaking the doll and ringing the bells, recite the Psalm 23 seven times.

Pinch out the candle but let incense burn out. Leave the candle and doll setup on your altar for the next day. Repeat for six more nights. Each night you may add a new paper of wants and needs and place it under the candle. On the last night of the spell, ring the bell seven times after chanting and let the candle finish burning down. Burn the petition papers in the final flames of the candle. Keep the doll in your home near where you keep your money or important financial papers, such as in a safe or drawer. Dispose of the wax remains and the ashes at a crossroads.

Voodoo Doll for Money

by Doktor Snake

If finances are tight, and you're having trouble paying your bills, the following Voodoo doll money spell will help bring in extra cash. The spell has the potential to bring in more money than you need, too—a happy situation!

The first thing you need to do is find a small silver coin. I favor old British sixpences because I live in the UK. But a silver dime would do fine. And I use silver dimes too because of my close connections with the U.S.

Once you've got your silver coin, you'll need a green Voodoo doll. Either make one or buy one. Sew your coin into the doll. Then anoint two green candles with Money-Drawing oil, and sprinkle some on the Voodoo doll as well.

Place the Voodoo doll between the two candles. Then light the candles and say a prayer along the following lines:

Spirits, bring me money, bring me cash,
Fill my coffers with the finances I need
To live a good and happy life!

Now snuff out the candles and go about your day, knowing that you'll have the money you need very soon. You can repeat this spell as often as you like, but three times a week should probably be the maximum.

Gypsy Money Doll

In one of the rare and now out-of-print publications by Finbarr International is written a spell described by a gypsy named *Magico* for making money dolls. Two dolls are needed for the spell, and, oddly enough, so is a statue or figure of a gnome. Apparently, the gnome represents wealth and prosperity and thus amplifies the intent of the spell. One doll is called the "priestess" doll and the other one is simply a green doll.

The book emphasizes that the dolls need not be sophisticated pieces of art; simple crude representations of human form will suffice. It is not the appearance of the dolls themselves that is important; rather, it is the magic in which you imbue them that is of import. Two crude representations of dolls are needed. The dolls can be made from two sticks, one crossing the other with two large beads for heads. One doll must have a gold head and the other doll must be green. Paint the bead on one doll with gold paint, unless you are using a large gold bead. Paint the head and body of the other doll green. The dolls need only be about three or four inches in size.

To harness the power needed to create magical dolls, you need to create the right energy in your environment. The room should be lit dimly, and you should be seated in front of a table or a working altar. Focus all of your thoughts on obtaining the wealth you desire. Having the correct discipline to control and focus your thoughts is central to creating powerful magic.

To charge the dolls magically, Magico directs the reader to draw a circle the size of a dinner plate on a large piece of paper and set the dolls in the center. Then, a petition is written inside the circle describing specifically what is needed. For example, "I will be debt-free and have $2,000 extra per month to do with what I will." Magico gives the examples "I wish to win 300 pounds to pay for so-and-so" and "I want to win the lottery in order to settle my debts and live a worry-free life." It is generally recommended that you keep petitions as realistic and specific as possible, as those petitions tend to manifest more easily. Obviously, Magico's gypsy mindset is such that reaching for the stars is attainable, so if you are trying this spell, write your petition however you like.

Light a white candle and focus on the petition. Magico does not state where to set the candle, so you will have to draw upon your own experience and tradition to determine where you will set the candle. I would recommend putting it inside the circle since we are working with sympathetic magic principles.

The next step is to pick up the green doll and whisper to it, "My name is [state your name] and I hold in my hand a fetish of an ancient god form." Hold the doll to your forehead and state: "I now release from my mind into this doll the magic of my own being. It is my will from this very moment that the power within this doll will bring to me that which is my birthright." Place the doll back on the table and have a brief period of meditation. Extinguish the candle and proceed as usual with your daily routine.

Magico explains that there are Universal laws designed to give people who follow them an advantage. Failure to live within these laws results in a life of misery, poverty, and failure. Living within these laws results in a happy, fulfilling, and prosperous life. What he describes is the *Law of Attraction*, a natural law based on the premise that "thoughts become things" and how we live, speak, and think brings us that which we want (or don't want, as it were).

Magico goes on to discuss the importance of getting rid of the old to make way for the new, which sounds like the law of reciprocity, though he doesn't state it as such. There is a give-and-take dynamic in the Universe that we can activate or stagnate, depending on our actions. Change is the natural state of things, and so we can work with the change and direct it through our thoughts and actions. It is the person's connection to the Universal Mind that brings about what appears to be the magic of a fetish doll as opposed to some inexplicable mystical attribute of a material object. The exchange of energy between petitioner and fetish doll makes the doll a magnet for attracting money and prosperity, with the petitioner's thoughts functioning as a magnet.

TEN

EMPLOYMENT SPELLS

Gain a Specific Job

Create a conjure doll out of green or gold fabric. Stuff with clover, chamomile, gravel root, blessed salt, ginger, nine pieces of Devil's Shoestring, and cinnamon. Insert a gold lodestone. Sprinkle a little gold lodestone food inside the poppet before stitching up. Anoint yourself and the doll with Steady Work oil. Obtain the logo, business card, or advertisement from the classifieds of the place where you want to work and anoint the four corners of the paper with Steady Work oil. Attach it to the doll. Fill out an application for employment and sprinkle Steady Work powder on the back of the application. Make sure the powder goes from the top to the bottom of the page by dragging your four fingers down through the powder, going side to side in a wavy motion. Lay the application on a table and place the doll on top of the application. If you do not have an application, write a petition for the job on a piece of paper. Be specific about the position you want, salary you need, and any other important details. Talk to the doll as if it were your potential employer and tell it why you're the best person for the job. Next, light a Steady Work vigil candle and say Psalm 23. Repeat daily (talking to the doll, lighting the candle, and praying the psalm) until the candle has burned down or you get the job.

Sacred Heart of Jesus Employment Spell

The Sacred Heart of Jesus is one of the most famous religious devotions to Jesus' physical heart as the representation of His divine love for humanity. The Sacred Heart is often depicted in Christian art as a flaming heart shining with divine light, pierced by the lance-wound, surrounded by a crown of thorns, surmounted by a cross, and bleeding. Sometimes the image is over Jesus' body with his wounded hands pointing at the heart. The wounds and crown of thorns allude to the manner of Jesus' death, while the fire represents the transformative power of love.

Create a Voodoo doll and attach an image of the Sacred Heart of Jesus to it. Anoint the doll daily with Steady Work oil while praying the Novena of the Sacred Heart.

Novena Prayer

Divine Jesus, You have said, "Ask and you shall receive; seek and you shall find; knock and it shall be opened to you." Behold me kneeling at Your feet, filled with a lively faith and confidence in the promises dictated by Your Sacred Heart to Saint Margaret Mary. I come to ask this favor: [Mention your request].

To whom can I turn if not to You, Whose Heart is the source of all graces and merits? Where should I seek if not in the treasure which contains all the riches of Your kindness and mercy? Where should I knock if not at the door through which God gives Himself to us and through which we go to God? I have recourse to You, Heart of Jesus. In You I find consolation when afflicted, protection when persecuted, strength when burdened with trials, and light in doubt and darkness.

Dear Jesus, I firmly believe that You can grant me the grace I implore, even though it should require a miracle. You have only to will it and my prayer will be granted. I admit that I am most unworthy of Your favors, but this is not a reason for me to be discouraged. You are the God of mercy, and You will not refuse a contrite heart. Cast upon me a look of mercy, I beg of You, and Your kind Heart will find in my miseries and weakness a reason for granting my prayer.

Sacred Heart, whatever may be Your decision with regard to my request, I will never stop adoring, loving, praising, and serving You. My Jesus, be pleased

*to accept this my act of perfect resignation to the decrees of Your adorable Heart,
which I sincerely desire may be fulfilled in and by me and all Your creatures
forever.*

*Grant me the grace for which I humbly implore You through the Immaculate Heart of Your most sorrowful Mother. You entrusted me to her as her child,
and her prayers are all-powerful with You. Amen.*

Follow the novena prayer with "I am the ALPHA and OMEGA, the Sacred Heart
of Jesus. I am employed."

Honey Boss Doll

By Carolina Dean

The Honey Boss doll is a doll made specifically to sweeten your boss to you so that
he or she will like you and want to favor you. At the same time, it contains herbs
and curios that many folks have long believed to give you the power to dominate
and control other individuals. In this way, the Honey Boss is a combination of a
honey-jar and a Boss-Fix all in one!

To reflect their dual nature, I often craft these dolls in a combination of pink
(for sweetness) and purple (for domination and control). Don't worry if your sewing skills aren't up to snuff—you can simply make your doll in either pink or purple.
However, if you make your doll in pink, you can include a small piece of purple
cloth inside the doll, or vice versa.

The fact that this spell is crafted in the form of a doll makes it much more
versatile than a simple honey-jar, which requires you to burn a candle on it several
times a week. The doll travels a lot easier than a honey-jar so it is likely that you
will be able to hide it in your purse, briefcase, locker, or desk at work where it will
be closer to the target and you can work it at your leisure.

To make your Honey Boss doll, you will need the following:

Doll
Stuffing
Target's personal concerns
Licorice root
Whole cloves

Fennel seeds
Five-finger grass

Begin by eliminating all distractions. Turn off the television and the radio, get comfortable in your sacred space, and make the doll. While crafting the doll, let your thoughts focus on your boss and how you want him or her to treat you. When you have crafted your doll, stuffed it with the herbs and personal concerns, and sewn it up, you will ritually name the doll.

To ritually name the doll, smoke incense, breathe life into the doll, and name him or her. For example:

"As God blew the breath of life into Adam, I breathe the breath of life into this doll. I name you (NAME) and now you are (NAME). All that I do to you, I now do to (NAME)"

When you feel that you have formed a strong connection in your mind between the doll and the individual, you will begin to talk to the doll at least once a day. Refer to the person by name as if you were actually speaking to him or her. Tell them exactly how you feel and what it is that you wish for them to say or do.

Reward the doll when it works for you by giving it a small offering. For example, if the person likes coffee, you may put a small drop of coffee on the doll's mouth.

If the individual does not respond to your commands, you may wish to punish it by withholding such treats and by sticking it through with pins. Tell the person that you are doing this because they are not obeying your commands and that only when they do as you wish will the pins be removed. When the individual responds to your spell, remove the pins and reward them with a special treat. This is similar to training a dog or small child. You want to reward good behavior and punish bad behavior.

It is very important to keep your word and remove the pins when the individual responds to your command; otherwise, you may confuse the doll and it will no longer work for you or it will take longer to achieve positive results again.

Once they achieve results, some people tend to stop working the doll. However, for results to be lasting, you will have to continually work your doll lest the individual revert back to his or her old negative ways.

ELEVEN

BETTER BUSINESS SPELLS

Better business spells pave the way to economic security. They can be used for bringing in more customers, influencing returns on investments, getting a better job or a promotion, or for general good luck regarding any business or financial venture. Business spells are considered to be in the class of prosperity spells because they are concerned with financial quality of life. According to occultists, spells of this nature are best performed during a waxing or full moon.

The spells in this section are from antiquity; this illustrates that past or present, thriving in the marketplace is a primary concern of daily life.

Greco-Roman Business Spell

Were there really Voodoo dolls in ancient Greece? Well, perhaps not as we know them, but dolls made for use in magic spells were produced en masse at a rate that would rival that of the New Orleans Voodoo doll tourist trade. Following is an example of an ancient Greco-Roman business spell. I have left the original translation intact.

Take orange beeswax and the juice of the aeria plant and of ground ivy and mix them and fashion a figure of Hermes having a hollow bottom, grasping in his left hand a Herald's Wand and in his right a small Bag. Write on Hieratic Papyrus these Names, and you will see Continuous Business:

CHAIO'CHEN OUTIBILMEMNOUO'TH ATRAUICH.

Give Income and Business to this place, because Psentebeth lives here.

Put the Papyrus inside the doll and fill in the hole with the same orange beeswax. Then hide the doll in a wall, at an inconspicuous place, and crown Him on the outside, and sacrifice to Him a cock, and make a Drink Offering of Egyptian Wine, and light for Him a Lamp that is not colored Red.[50]

Little Beggar Charm Doll for Bringing in Customers

Here is another ancient Greek formula for a little charm doll made for the purpose of drawing in business and new customers. The doll is to be placed in the home, place of business, workshop, or wherever it is needed. The spell is ancient, remember, and calls for the sacrifice of a donkey, which is to be essentially roasted over an open fire and eaten while celebrating. If you decide to attempt to recreate this spell, try having a barbeque instead.

According to the papyri:[51] "By having it, you will become rich, you will be successful. For Hermes made this for the wandering Isis.[52] The charm is marvelous and is called 'the little beggar.'"

Take beeswax that has not been heated, which is known as bee glue, and fashion a man having his right arm in the position of begging and having in his

---

50. *The Greek Magical Papyri in Translation, Including the Demotic Spells*, Volume 1, Hans Dieter Betz, Ed. (Chicago: University of Chicago Press).

51. Roger Tomlin, *Tabellae Sulis: Roman Inscribed Tablets of Tin and Lead from the Sacred Spring at Bath* (1988).

52. Betz (1997) notes the wandering of Isis and refers to her as the widow of Osiris searching for his body. See Plutarch *De Is.et OS*, 14, 356D-E; 39, 366F, and Griffiths, *Plutarch's De Iside et Osiride* 315, 452, as cited in H.D. Betz (1997). *The Greek Magical Papyri in Translation, Including the Demotic Spells, Vol. I*, (Chicago: University of Chicago Press).

left a bag and a staff. Let there be around the staff a coiled snake, like Isis. Stand it up and erect it in a single block of hollowed out juniper, and have an asp covering the top as a capital. Fashion him during a new moon, and consecrate it in a celebrating mood, and read aloud the spell over his members, after you have divided him into three sections—repeating the spell four times for each member. For each member write on strips of papyrus made from a priestly scroll, with ink of cinnabar, juice of wormwood, and myrrh. When you have set it up high on the place you have chosen, sacrifice to it a wild ass with a white forehead and offer it whole and roast the inward parts over the wood of willow and thus eat it.

Now this is what is to be written on each strip of papyrus. Then spell on the bag:

EPH EROUCHIŌ CHŌRAI DARIDA MĒTHEUEI ABACHTHIE
EMESIE ECHENĒ IAE IEN EBAPS PHNEŌA ETHŌNICHAENTHA
TROMOCHMOUSŌ THERAŌCHEIN SASI SAMACHIŌTH OUASA
AMAKARALA KAIŌS LASOI.

Upon the head:
ŌAI IĒ ĒIĒ NAŌ OULABETHEN THERMATH ENESIE.

Upon the neck:
THALAA MEMARACHŌ CHETH THROU PHEN PHTHAI.

On the right shoulder:
ĒMAA CHNA THOUE BŌLERI.

On the left:
ARAIAŌ IĒE SYPSO ITHEN BACHTHIPHĒRPSOI THENIBON

On the belly:
AMAMAMAR AIII OU MAMŌ MAO OMBA.

On the sacred bone:
LANOA PHTHOUTHO OTHOM MATHATHOU.

On the right thigh:
ARIN THEA RAGNI MĒTHETHIŌ CHRĒ IĒ ERE.

On the left thigh:
ĒI ĒIN YEAIŌ ERENPS TEPHĒT PARAOU ANĒI.

On the private parts:
ĒERŌTHĒSONĒEN THNIBITH EUECHEN

On the right shin:
MIANIKOUĒI BIOUS

On the left shin:
CHNOU TOUŌYMOUCHOS ONIŌ

Under the sole of the right foot:
OURANION

Under the sole of the left foot:
ANOUPSIE

On the back of the buttocks:
ETEMPSIS PSPHOPS IAIAĒĒIOO

On the snake the name AGATHOS DIAMON, *which is, as Epaphroditus says the following:* PHRĒ ANOI PHRŌCHŌ PHYYY RORPSIS OROCHŌŌI, *but as on the paper which I found the spell was changed thus,* Harponknouphi *(formula).*

This is the spell for the rite:

I receive you as the cowherd who has his camp toward the south, I receive you for the widow and the orphan. Therefore, give me favor, work for my business. Bring to me silver, gold, clothing, much wealth for the good of it. (Translation: R.F. Hock)[53]

---

53. *The Greek Magical Papyri in Translation, Including the Demotic Spells*, Volume 1, Hans Dieter Betz, Ed. (Chicago: University of Chicago Press).

Paper Voodoo doll created by the author for Manman Brigit,
the Vodou loa of the cemeteries and money.

COURT CASE SPELLS

Aside form love spells, money spells, and spells of revenge, court case spells are among the most frequently requested by my customers. Court case spells are reportedly useful for all types of legal matters, from traffic tickets to lawsuits to incarcerations. Just remember that magick is not a substitute for sound legal advice or representation, so make sure you do the best you can with the resources at your disposal, and use magick as an adjunct reinforcer.

Release a Prisoner

Light a brown candle. Create a Voodoo doll out of black-and-white striped material. Alternatively, you can use a strip of black and a strip of white material and wrap around the doll figure so that the colors alternate as stripes. Find out the names of the judge, prosecuting attorney, and the jurors on the case and write them down on a piece of parchment paper. Tuck the name paper securely inside the doll. Then, take the doll and soak it in cold water for nine minutes. Place the wet doll in the freezer overnight.

The next morning, take the frozen Voodoo doll out of the freezer and sprinkle with powdered sugar. Arrange nine black candles around the Voodoo doll and light them. Lay the Voodoo doll on the floor and lie down on the floor in front of the Voodoo doll. Recite Psalm 102.

Psalm 102

Hear my prayer, O LORD, and let my cry come unto thee.

*Hide not thy face from me in the day when I am in trouble; incline thine ear
    unto me: in the day when I call answer me speedily.*

For my days are consumed like smoke, and my bones are burned as an hearth.

My heart is smitten, and withered like grass; so that I forget to eat my bread.

By reason of the voice of my groaning my bones cleave to my skin.

I am like a pelican of the wilderness: I am like an owl of the desert.

I watch, and am as a sparrow alone upon the house top.

*Mine enemies reproach me all the day; and they that are mad against me are
    sworn against me.*

For I have eaten ashes like bread, and mingled my drink with weeping.

*Because of thine indignation and thy wrath: for thou hast lifted me up, and
    cast me down.*

My days are like a shadow that declineth; and I am withered like grass.

*But thou, O LORD, shall endure for ever; and thy remembrance unto all gen-
    erations.*

*Thou shalt arise, and have mercy upon Zion: for the time to favour her, yea, the
    set time, is come.*

For thy servants take pleasure in her stones, and favour the dust thereof.

*So the heathen shall fear the name of the LORD, and all the kings of the earth
    thy glory.*

When the LORD shall build up Zion, he shall appear in his glory.

He will regard the prayer of the destitute, and not despise their prayer.

*This shall be written for the generation to come: and the people which shall be
    created shall praise the LORD.*

*For he hath looked down from the height of his sanctuary; from heaven did the
    LORD behold the earth;*

To hear the groaning of the prisoner; to loose those that are appointed to death;

To declare the name of the LORD in Zion, and his praise in Jerusalem;
When the people are gathered together, and the kingdoms, to serve the LORD.
He weakened my strength in the way; he shortened my days.
I said, O my God, take me not away in the midst of my days: thy years are
throughout all generations.
Of old hast thou laid the foundation of the earth: and the heavens are the work
of thy hands.
They shall perish, but thou shalt endure: yea, all of them shall wax old like a
garment; as a vesture shalt thou change them, and they shall be changed:
But thou art the same, and thy years shall have no end.
The children of thy servants shall continue, and their seed shall be established
before thee.[54]

Wrap the doll in clean white cloth and keep in a safe place until the prisoner is released. Once he or she is released, place the doll in a brown paper sack and toss in a moving river or leave at a crossroads.

Make a Judge Sick

Take a black candle and melt it down to soften the wax. Form a human figure out of the wax by coating your hands with a few drops of Dragon's Blood conjure oil and molding a human shape out of the softened wax. You can add hair or nail clippings or some other personal effect of the person who the doll represents. Write the judge's name on a piece of parchment paper with Dragon's Blood ink or a red ink pen if you don't have the Dragon's Blood ink. Place the paper into the wax and cover the paper with more wax. When you have your figure formed and the paper well sealed inside, place the doll into a bowl of cold water. The day before the court date, take a stick and spin the doll around in the water all day long. The judge should fail to show for court the following day.

---

54. Scripture quotations taken from the 21st Century King James Version, copyright 1994. Used by permission of Deuel Enterprises, Inc., Gary, SD 57237. All rights reserved.

Formula for Dragon's Blood Conjure Oil

Dragon's Blood resin (powdered)
Gum arabic

Mix equal amounts of the above to two ounces of olive oil to which a small amount of vitamin E has been added as a preservative.

Ochosi Spell for Justice

Ochosi is the African orisha that represents the forces of nature and is one of the three warrior orishas referred to as the "Ibori" in the Yoruba religion. He is the patron of justice, prisoners, and the accused, and is a divine hunter, fisherman, and tracker. Ochosi is also a great magician and seer. This spell is particularly effective for avoiding problems with the court.

For this spell, you will need to make or purchase a Voodoo doll that represents Ochosi. Ochosi's colors are yellow and blue and he is always depicted as a hunter wearing animal skins. Set your Ochosi doll on a small table you can make into an altar. Place a bow and arrow on the table along with a photo of St. Norbert. Write on a piece of parchment paper the names of everyone involved in the case, including the judge if known. Make sure you specify who is who. Place three rooster feathers, three pieces of dried fruit, three hairs from a dog and three hairs from a cat, and a piece of John the Conqueror root in the center of the paper. Roll everything up in the paper and secure with a piece of leather.

Say the following prayer to St. Norbert:

Prayer for Protection against Enemies and for Justice:

Blessed San Norberto, since you belong
Chosen to the Celestial Father to hunt the good things and to remove the bad
*   things,*
Since you are the proprietor of jails and prisons, close the doors so that I never
*   have to enter them again.*
To you, the Most glorious San Norberto, I beg your help and I ask you to re-
*   move with your three arrows illnesses, sudden death, treachery, accidents,*
*   and enemies from my life. Always cover me with your Divine power*

guided by the Divine Hand completely powerfully and glorious
Virgin Mary.

Bury the bundle in the ground near the courthouse. Then take three fresh pieces of fruit and leave them in the forest under a tree while stating your request to Ochosi.

THIRTEEN

SPELLS FOR GOOD LUCK, SUCCESS, & GAMBLING

Good luck and success spells are designed to bring success, luck, and recognition in all of your endeavors. If you need a boost in school or your job, or if you are seeking to improve your lot in life, remove bad luck, and draw good energy, then a good luck and success spell can give you the added confidence you need to succeed.

Although good luck and success spells can be performed at any time, occultists generally agree that the best times to do such spells are during a waxing or full moon.

General Good Luck Spell

For this spell, you will need a Voodoo doll to represent yourself in whatever color you think appropriate, a white candle, a black candle, and a green candle. Hold the doll that represents you and say: "I am this doll and this doll is me. I name you (state your name)." Light the black candle and say: "This candle represents all the bad luck and negative energy surrounding me. As I light this candle and the candle burns, so shall the bad luck and negativity leave." Light the white candle and say: "May light and healing surround me." Light the green candle and say: "This is the

positive energy coming my way, good luck in matters of money, love, and employment [and whatever else you want luck in]."

Sit quietly holding the doll and visualize bad luck dissolving before your eyes
and being replaced by only good, positive things. When the candles have burned
down completely, the spell is done. Dispose of the wax remains at a crossroads and
bury the doll in a garden of beautiful flowers.

Good Luck Charm Doll

Make a doll baby out of green or yellow fabric. Stuff with seven different good luck
herbs such as alfalfa, mint, basil, and rose petals. Add a pair of gold lodestones,
three acorns, and a lock of your hair. Sew the doll closed, and attach as many good
luck charms as you can to the outside. Bless the doll under a full moon every month
of the year to ensure success in all areas of your life.

Lucky Conjure Doll

Create a conjure doll to bring you good mojo, drive away evil, and attract good
luck and success. Make a Voodoo poppet out of yellow flannel and stuff with three
black-eyed peas, a piece of John the Conqueror root, a chunk of Dragon's Blood
resin, two lodestones with a little gold magnetic sand, and five finger grass. Sew
it closed. Add two buttons for eyes and sew or draw a smile on its face. Hang an
evil eye bead on a string around its neck. Every Friday, anoint the top of your head
with Crown of Success oil and do the same with your conjure doll. Keep your lucky
conjure doll in your living room where it can bless all who enter with good luck.

Formula for Crown of Success Oil

Use the essential oils or essences for the ingredients listed. The dried herbs can be
used in place of oil or as an adjunct to the oil.

Orange essential oil
Allspice essential oil
Ambergris oil
7 whole allspice berries

Add the above ingredients to a one-ounce base of sunflower oil to which a small amount of vitamin E has been added. Add a pinch of gold glitter to the bottle.

You may adjust the above formula to suit your needs.

Gambling Spells

Lucky charms such as Voodoo dolls, rabbit feet, and other objects have been used for hundreds of years by people looking to get lucky in love, business, or most often, when gambling. Whether you're playing online at Internet gambling, going to a casino, or playing bingo, craps, or picking lotto numbers, you will naturally seek any and all means at your disposal to increase your odds at winning. Hoodoo in particular has a whole host of products and magickal works geared towards winning games of chance. The magickal doll spells that follow combine hoodoo herbal lore and curios with doll baby conjure to help you gain the edge at gambling.

Fast Luck Buckeye Voodoo Doll Spell

Buckeye nuts have been used as good luck charms for years. The name "Buckeye" came from the Native Americans, who noticed that the glossy, chestnut-brown seeds with the lighter circular "eye" looked very similar to the eye of a buck (male) deer. My mother always told me that buckeyes were lucky and she always kept one in her purse and told me to carry one in my pocket. In hoodoo, it is believed that carrying a buckeye in one's pocket will bring good luck and increase pocket money. Lucky buckeyes were carried in men's pockets, sometimes for their entire lives. They are coveted by gamblers, who anoint them with Fast Luck oil and carry them concealed in their mojo bags for luck in games of chance.

It seems that the buckeye has medicinal properties, too. Early travelers carried buckeye nuts with them because they believed in their ability to help with spinal treatments, pain associated with rheumatism, headaches, male virility (because of their resemblance to testicles, I am told), and arthritis.

For this spell, make a green or yellow doll baby and stuff it with any six money-drawing herbs, such as green Irish moss, cinnamon chips, five finger grass, alfalfa, cloves, and ginger. Add the hair of a black cat (do not hurt a cat to get its fur). Place a buckeye nut in the head. Anoint with Fast Luck oil. Wrap the doll with gold thread and tie a pair of dice onto the doll. Each time you go to play the lottery or to gamble, pour a few drops of Fast Luck oil in the palms of your hands and rub them together quickly, creating heat from the friction. Then, pick up your lucky doll and hold it close to your pocket, visualizing your pockets filled with money.

The buckeye gambling doll pictured, "Buck-Eye Joe" is a variation of this doll. I made this doll in the sticks and moss style and glued a buckeye to the top of the stem for the head. I further secured the nut to the sticks by wrapping the fabric around the nut and down the stem. Then I painted the face to resemble cowry shells for features.

Formula for Fast Luck Oil

Use the essential oils or essences for the ingredients listed. The dried herbs can be used in place of oil or as an adjunct to the oil.

Cinnamon essential oil
Vanilla essential oil
Patchouli essential oil
Wintergreen essential oil

Combine seven drops of each of the above oils in one ounce of almond oil to which a small amount of vitamin E has been added as a preservative. To get the characteristic red color found in Algiers formulas, add just a few flakes of alkanet root.

The above formula and its proportions are just suggestions; you may adjust to suit your needs.

Lucky Gambling Voodoo Doll

On a piece of chamois, write the amount of money you want to win in Dove's Blood ink. Make a doll baby out of red flannel and stick the chamois inside the doll. Wrap the doll in red flannel and tuck a shark's tooth inside the first wrap (layer one) and pine sap in the second wrap (second layer). Anoint with Fast Luck oil. Rub the doll before gambling for good luck.

THE VOODOO DOLL SPELLBOOK

Simple Formula for Dove's Blood Ink

Red ink
Rose essential oil

Add a few drops of rose essential oil or fragrance oil to the ink and write with a feather quill.

Wheel of Fortune Voodoo Doll Baby

This spell will require the use of the Wheel of Fortune tarot card image from the deck of your choice. It also calls for some of the classic New Orleans conjure oil for good luck, Has No Hanna. This oil is great for those folks who have trouble holding on to their money, paying bills on time, or sticking to a budget. Gamblers are known to use this oil before gambling by anointing their money, wallets, and good luck charms. You will need the following items:

Gold fabric
A pair of gold lodestones
Gold magnetic sand (lodestone food)
Shredded money
3 black-eyed peas
A piece of pyrite
A whole nutmeg
Irish moss
A pair of dice beads
A key
Has No Hanna conjure oil
A gold candle

Create your doll baby out of the gold fabric and stuff with the green Irish moss and shredded money. Before sewing closed, insert the piece of pyrite, two gold lodestones, and three black-eyed peas, and sprinkle some gold lodestone food inside the doll. Now, sew the doll closed. Next, sew the two dice on the doll for eyes to reflect how you want the dice to roll. Then, sew on the key for the mouth of the doll.

Now, lay the Wheel of Fortune card on a table or surface you have prepared for magick work. Lay your gold Voodoo doll on top of the card. Anoint the gold candle with Has No Hanna oil and set the candle at the head of the doll. Light the candle and recite Psalm 23 three times. Allow the candle to burn all the way down. Bury the wax remains along with the Wheel of Fortune card in a potted jade plant kept by the entrance of your home. Keep your doll where you keep your money at home and any time you need a boost of luck, anoint a gold candle with Has No Hanna oil and recite Psalm 23 three times. When performing this ritual again, bury the wax remains in your yard.

Psalm 23

The LORD is my shepherd; I shall not want.
He maketh me to lie down in green pastures: he leadeth me beside the
*   still waters.*
He restoreth my soul: he leadeth me in the paths of righteousness for his
*   name's sake.*
Yea, though I walk through the valley of the shadow of death, I will fear no
*   evil: for thou art with me; thy rod and thy staff they comfort me.*
Thou preparest a table before me in the presence of mine enemies: thou anointest
*   my head with oil; my cup runneth over.*
Surely goodness and mercy shall follow me all the days of my life: and I will
*   dwell in the house of the LORD for ever.*[55]

---

55. Scripture quotations taken from the 21st Century King James Version, copyright 1994. Used by permission of Deuel Enterprises, Inc., Gary, SD 57237. All rights reserved.

The Voodoo Doll Spellbook

Formula for Has No Hanna Conjure Oil

Use the essential oils or essences for the ingredients listed. The dried herbs can be used in place of oil or as an adjunct to the oil.

Jasmine essential oil
Cinnamon essential oil
Mint leaves

Add thirteen drops of jasmine essential oil and five drops of oil of cinnamon in a one-ounce base of almond oil to which a small amount of vitamin E has been added. Add a pinch of mint leaves to the oil.

The above formula (and its proportions) is just one formula; you may adjust ingredients to suit your needs.

BLESSING, HEALING AND FERTILITY SPELLS

Magick rituals can be great adjuncts to other healing methods. They provide hope, nourishment for the spirit, and offer a sense of control when a person feels as if they have none. Healing spells are best performed during a waxing or full moon.

Please note that none of the spells in this section are a substitute for medical treatment of any illness, disease, or injury.

Cure-All Poppet

Try making the following doll for whatever ails you. Create a white poppet and stuff it with Jimson weed, sulfur, and sugar. Find a black cat with one white foot and rub the poppet against the cat. Keep the poppet in your pillow until you are well.

Healing Poppet

This is a healing ritual that is to be used with a white doll baby. You can make a poppet-style doll and fill with healing herbs like agrimony, acacia, sage, and hyssop and add some blessed resins like myrrh, frankincense, and copal. Add a taglock from the person in need of healing to the doll. Then, anoint with a healing oil of your choice.

You can use the image below as a template to make your doll baby . . . just be sure it is white.

The first thing you will do is a baptism/consecration/naming ritual. You will name the doll using the name of the person to be healed.

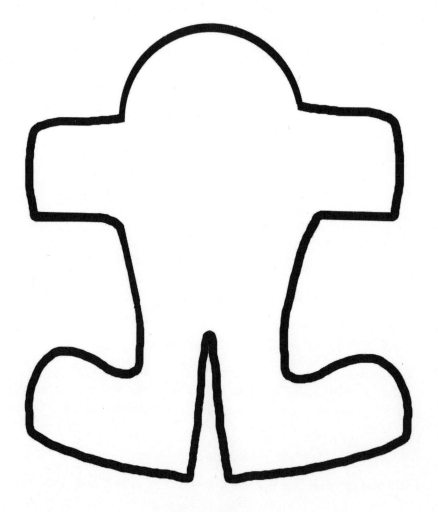

Doll baby pattern.

THE VOODOO DOLL SPELLBOOK

The act of consecration involves opening up to and tapping into the Universal Divine force from which all possibilities, solutions, and miracles emanate. To consecrate an object for ritual use is to connect to this Universal Divine force and declare sacred or appropriate for sacred use the object at hand.

Consecrating an object removes any negativity that may be attached to the object and purifies it. It removes the vibrational energies of anyone who has handled the object other than you. This is the foundation of any effective magick or ceremonial work.

Next, you will need to set up an altar. This should be a special place free of clutter and any objects other than what you will be using for the ritual. It can be a small table, a dresser top, a shelf, or any similar place. Drape a clean white cloth over the altar.

Write out your petition, stating exactly what you want, and place it in the middle of the cloth. Pour about a half a pound of sugar in a mound on top of the petition. Sugar is used as a "sweetener" in Voodoo and hoodoo for spells in which you want to draw something to you, in this case healing and affection. Spread the sugar out just enough so that the doll will be able to lie on it from head to toe. Pour the healing herbs on top of the sugar and spread them out. Lay the doll carefully on the bed of sugar and herbs. Be sure to talk to the doll as if you are talking to your loved one. Tell her you have prepared this wonderful bed of healing herbs for her and you are laying her on the bed so that she will feel better and so she can rest.

Take the fixed white candle and make nine notches in it, equal spaces apart. You will be doing this spell nine days in a row and allowing it to burn to one notch each day. Place the candle on the altar at the head of the doll and light it. Place the incense at the foot of the doll and light it. Then say the following prayer:

> Blessed is the doll of light who is pure in heart,
>> for you shall see the Divine.
> For as the heavens give you the Holy Spirit,
>> and your Mother Earth has given you her holy body,
> so shall you radiate health and well-being, physically, spiritually, mentally, and
>> emotionally.
> Let your love be as the Sun
> which shines on all the creatures of the earth,
> and does not favor one blade of grass for another.

And this love shall flow as a fountain from person to person and to me as your
loved one,
and as it is spent so shall it be replenished.
For love is eternal.
Love is stronger than the currents of deep waters.
Love is stronger than death.
And we have love,
When walls which have been built are knocked down
Image of cloth, you are born whole and healthy
I bestow upon you the name [name].
Their body is your body
Their mind is your mind,
Their soul is your soul,
You are as One under Divine Law.
Amen.

With the anointing oil, anoint the top of the doll's head and visualize your loved one as healthy and energetic. When the candle has burned down to the first notch, pinch out the flame with your thumb and index finger (do not blow it out). After the incense has burned down, keep the ashes near the mound and take one end of the cloth and pull it over the doll as if you are putting her to bed. Do NOT cover her face (this would change the entire meaning of the ritual).

Each day, take down her covers and light the candle and incense. Address the doll by name and tell her she is whole and healthy and pray Psalm 103:1-3:

Bless the Lord, O my soul, and all that is within me, bless his holy name. Bless the Lord, O my soul, and forget not all his benefits: Who forgives all thine iniquities, who heals all thy diseases.

Anoint the doll with the anointing oil and repeat for nine days in a row.

Doll Baby Spell for Healing

Make a doll baby out of white fabric that has been prewashed in water infused with hyssop. Stuff it with sage and cedar. Insert a piece of frankincense (for the Father), a piece of myrrh (Son), and a piece of gold jewelry or pyrite (the Holy Ghost). On a piece of parchment paper, write the name of the person you want to heal. Stick the name paper inside the doll and stitch the doll closed. Attach a photo of the sick person to the doll where the doll's face should be. Insert a white pin into the area in need of healing. Light a white candle and pray Psalm 6:2 followed by a heartfelt prayer of your own.

Have mercy upon me (or the name of the patient), O Lord, for I (he/she) am (is) weak: O Lord, heal me (name), for my (their) bones are vexed.

Repeat daily until the patient is healed.

To Heal a Sick Person

Create a poppet out of white fabric or unbleached muslin. While making the poppet, focus on what needs to be healed. Stuff the poppet with hyssop, Angelica, agrimony, and sage, and add pieces of frankincense and myrrh. Attach a personal item that belongs to the person in need of healing to the poppet. Create a small circle with four quadrants out of white cornmeal on an altar draped with a white cloth. Lay the poppet in the center of the circle. Place a white candle at the head of the doll and one at the foot of the doll. Place a crucifix on the doll and splash it with holy water. As you do this, you should be focusing all of your thoughts on healing the ailment in question. Light the candles and let them burn for nine minutes each day for nine days in a row while reciting a healing prayer of your choice. On the ninth day, allow the candles to burn down and dispose of the wax remains in a running river.

White Voodoo Doll to Hasten Healing

To move along the healing process when someone is sick, create a Voodoo doll out of white fabric. Attach the name of the person to be healed to the doll with a white pin. Attach some of the person's hair to the head of the doll. Lay the doll on top of a clean white cloth, and set two white candles on either side of the doll. Anoint the candles and the doll with Healing oil, and then light both candles. Say a prayer for healing. Allow the candles to burn all the way down. Then wrap the doll in the white cloth and tend to it daily as you would the person who is sick.

Formula for Healing Oil

Use the essential oils or essences for the ingredients listed. The dried herbs can be used in place of oil or as an adjunct to the oil.

> *Oil of thyme*
> *Myrrh gum*
> *Benzoin*

Add the above ingredients to a one-ounce base of olive oil to which a small amount of vitamin E has been added. Add a piece of myrrh gum to the bottle.

You may adjust these ingredients to suit your needs.

Sheela Na-Gig Doll for Fertility

By Carolina Dean

Sheela Na-gig doll. Photo courtesy of Carolina Dean.

Sheela na-gig is the name for a type of carving that depicts an exotic and unusual woman displaying her exaggeratedly large vulva. Though these carvings can be found all over Europe, they are most numerous in Ireland where they can be found on churches and ancient castles as well as hanging over the doors of modern homes and businesses.

Many theories have been put forth concerning the etymology of her name as well as the Sheela na-gig's symbolism and purpose. One theory suggests that *Sheela na-gig* means "Sheela of the breasts" while another proposes that its meaning is "Sheela on her hunkers." To date, however, no definitive answer has been forthcoming.

Similarly, the exact symbolism and meaning of the Sheela's posture have been a source of debate over the years. There are three main theories about the figure's purpose and meaning. They are:

A symbol of fertility and childbirth: Though modern academics have rejected the notion, many folks believe that the figure represents an ancient Irish fertility goddess. Because some Sheela na-gig are shown with male counterparts, these figures are often associated with marriage and fertility rites. In some areas of Ireland images of the Sheela na-gig are placed under the heads of women giving birth in the hopes that this will ease the pain of childbirth.

A warning against lust: Other folks believe that the Sheela na-gig represents a religious warning against the sin of lust. Historically, women were considered the "weaker sex" and therefore more apt to succumb to the temptation of the flesh. The Sheela was a warning of what they could become if they allowed themselves to be overcome with lust.

Protection from evil: Women's bodies have been both reviled and worshipped throughout history. A greater part of that history is the objectification of their bodies and the idea that their genitals and the products thereof (i.e., menstruation) are somehow *unclean* or *evil*. Therefore, like gargoyles and other grotesques, the female vulva came to be a symbol of protection from evil. For this reason, they are often hung over doorways to bar the entrance of evil spirits.

How to Make Your Own Sheela Na-Gig

Making your own Sheela na-gig need not be a complicated exercise. To make your own, you will need:

Salt dough
Human-shaped cookie cutter
Cowrie shells
Paint (optional)

Begin with your basic salt dough. You can use it as it is or you can add protective herbs in their powdered form. Roll the dough out flat. Using the human-shaped cookie cutter, cut out several figures and lay them aside. Gently press the cowrie shells into the dough and simply allow it to dry. Once the figure is dry, you may want to paint it a grayish color to mimic a stone figure and then add several coats of clear varnish for preservation.

You can dress the figure with any number of protection oils and pray to Sheela na-gig to safeguard your home and all that lies within. Finally, hang the figure over the outside of your front door to act as a watcher and protector. Much like a Mezuzah, many folks who keep a Sheela na-gig above their door make a habit of touching the figure for luck as they enter or leave the home.

The Blessing Spell

The following spell is for bringing blessings and healing into your home, self, and space. The spell can help you gain the assistance of the saints, helper spirits, and personal and archetypal ancestors. You can do a blessing for yourself at any time; in fact, it is a good idea to perform some sort of blessing regularly as a sort of spiritual maintenance. Any blessing work will raise the spiritual vibrations in your home and is highly protective.

While blessings can be done at any time, if you want to remove evil and negativity, occultists say that the best time to perform such a blessing is on a Sunday under a waning or full moon.

Our Lady of Good Remedy Doll

This Voodoo doll spell is appropriate for any problem you may be having, whether it be physical, emotional, financial, or spiritual. It is especially suited to those times when asking for help is difficult. Invoke the assistance of Our Lady of Good Remedy, and you will surely experience the power of her intercession.

Create a white Voodoo doll in the style and material of your choice. Stuff the doll with dollar bills of any denomination, New Orleans Lucky Green Rice, sage, mugwort, balm of Gilead, hyssop, bay laurel, vetivert, and a cross. Attach a photo of the person in need of help to the front of the doll with a pin with a white head, and make sure that the face you draw or sew on the doll is wearing a smile. If you do not have a photo, write the name of the person on parchment paper and attach to the doll with a white-headed pin.

Lay the doll on a clean white cloth and anoint with All Saints oil. All Saints oil is a potent, African-inspired anointing oil used for healing, success, uncrossing, and when the intercession of the highest spirits is warranted. Anoint two white candles with All Saints oil and place one at the head of the doll and the other at the foot of the doll. When anointing the candles, be sure to spread the oil towards you rather than away from you, because you want to draw help to you. Light the candles each day for about fifteen minutes for nine days in a row, and pray the novena to Our Lady of Good Remedy. A novena is a Catholic tradition where one prayer or a group of prayers is recited for nine consecutive days for special intentions and petitions. The praying of a novena draws its origin from the practice of the disciples, who prayed for the nine days between the ascension of Jesus and the arrival of the Holy Spirit at Pentecost.[56]

Novena to Our Lady of Good Remedy

QUEEN OF HEAVEN and earth, Most Holy Virgin, we venerate thee. Thou art the beloved Daughter of the Most High God, the chosen Mother of the Incarnate Word, the Immaculate Spouse of the Holy Spirit, the Sacred Vessel of the Most Holy Trinity.

---

56. "Catholic Prayers: Novena for the Intercession of St. Faustina," http://www.scborromeo.org/prayers/faustinanovena.pdf.

Mother of the Divine Redeemer, who under the title of Our Lady of Good Remedy comes to the aid of all who call upon thee, extend thy maternal protection to us. We depend on thee, Dear Mother, as helpless and needy children depend on a tender and caring mother.

Pray: Hail Mary

Hail Mary, Full of grace
The Lord is with thee
Blessed art thou among women
And blessed is the fruit of thy womb Jesus
Holy Mary, Mother of God
Pray for our sinners
Now and in the hour of our death, Amen.

LADY OF GOOD REMEDY, source of unfailing help, grant that we may
      draw from thy treasury of graces in our time of need.
Touch the hearts of sinners, that they may seek reconciliation and forgiveness.
Bring comfort to the afflicted and the lonely; help the poor and the hopeless; aid the sick and the suffering. May they be healed in body and strengthened in spirit to endure their sufferings with patient resignation and Christian fortitude.

Pray: Hail Mary

DEAR LADY OF GOOD REMEDY, source of unfailing help, thy compassionate heart knows a remedy for every affliction and misery we encounter in life. Help me with thy prayers and intercession to find a remedy for my problems and needs, especially for . . . [Here indicate your special intentions].

On my part, O loving Mother, I pledge myself to a more intensely Christian lifestyle, to a more careful observance of the laws of God, to be more conscientious in fulfilling the obligations of my state in life, and to strive to be a source of healing in this broken world of ours.

*Dear Lady of Good Remedy, be ever present to me, and through thy interces-
sion, may I enjoy health of body and peace of mind, and grow stronger in the
faith and in the love of thy Son, Jesus.*

Pray: Hail Mary

*Pray for us, O Holy Mother of Good Remedy, That we may deepen our dedica-
tion to thy Son, and make the world alive with His Spirit.*

On the final day of ritual, allow the candles to burn all the way down. Dispose of
the wax remains at a crossroads, and wrap the doll in the white cloth and keep it
in a safe place. Repeat every month as desired, using the same doll if for the same
person and purpose.

Formula for All Saints Oil

Use the essential oils or essences for the ingredients listed. The dried herbs can be
used in place of oil or as an adjunct to the oil.

Oil of cinnamon
Tonka bean
Patchouli essential oil
Vanilla essential oil
Lavender essential oil
Gardenia perfume oil

Add equal amounts of the above ingredients to two ounces of olive oil to which a
small amount of vitamin E has been added.

New Orleans Voodoo Doll for Blessings

Create a Voodoo doll baby out of red flannel. Place the following ingredients inside
the doll:

Fava bean

9 red beans (cut in halves)
One teaspoon of allspice
One teaspoon of parsley flakes
A small lock of your hair (or hair from the person for which the doll is made)
One jellyfish, sun dried and powdered
Flax seed

Each Friday as the sun sets, pour a little rum over the doll. Then, make a sign of the cross and concentrate on the blessings you need. The effects are said to be immediate.

BORNEO HEALING DOLL

In certain western districts of Borneo, if a man is suddenly and violently sick, the physician, who in this part of the world is generally an old woman, fashions a wooden image and touches it to the sufferer's head while she says: "This image serves to take the place of the sick man; sickness, pass over into the image." Then, with some rice, salt, and tobacco in a little basket, the substitute is carried to the spot where the evil spirit is supposed to have entered into the man. There it is set upright on the ground, after the physician has invoked the spirit as follows: "O devil, here is an image which stands instead of the sick man. Release the soul of the sick man and plague the image, for it is indeed prettier and better than he." Batak magicians can conjure the demon of disease out of a patient's body into an image made out of a banana tree with a human face and wrapped up in magic herbs; the image is then hurriedly removed and thrown away or buried beyond the boundaries of the village. Sometimes the image, dressed as a man or a woman according to the sex of the patient, is deposited at a crossroads or other thoroughfare, in the hope that some passerby, seeing it, may start and cry out, "Ah! So-and-so is dead." Such an exclamation is supposed to delude the demon of disease into a belief that he has accomplished his fell purpose, so he takes himself off and leaves the sufferer to get well.[57]

57. Frazer, J. G. (1912). *The Golden Bough*, New York and London: MacMillan and Co.

FIFTEEN

SPELLS FOR
POWER & DOMINATION

Spells for power and domination are among the unholy trinity of spells of this nature; the other two are commanding and controlling spells. Power and domination spells are performed to gain control and influence over people and situations, humiliate someone, promote mental powers, and feel empowered. If you are tired of passively submitting to the personal, societal, physical, mystical, or psychological forces around you, then consider one of the following spells.

Damballah Wedo Do as I Say Spell

The snake is highly revered in New Orleans Voodoo, and most Voodoo temples and houses possess their own boa constrictor or python used for ceremonial purposes. Marie Laveaux publicly danced with her snake, known as Li Grande Zombi, in what is now Congo Square in New Orleans. The snake is called upon for many purposes, including transformation, transcendence, ancestral knowledge, righteous retribution, and wisdom. Damballah Wedo is likened to St. Patrick, the Catholic patron saint of Ireland.

This spell is designed to help you sway a person in a particular direction. Here are the items needed for this spell:

One piece of ribbon each in red, yellow, and black
Photo of the person you want to do your bidding attached to a red Voodoo doll
High John the Conqueror root
Damballah Wedo oil

Take the three pieces of ribbon—one red, one yellow, and one black. Tie them together at one end and then knot them nine times. Each time you tie a knot, repeat the name of the person you are trying to influence.

Create a doll from red flannel and attach a photo of the person you are trying to influence. If you do not have a photo, then write the person's name nine times on a piece of brown paper with Dragon's Blood ink and attach it to the doll. Insert a piece of High John the Conqueror root and the ribbon tied with nine knots.

Draw the ritual symbol for Damballah and place it on a small table you have dedicated to this work. Alternatively, you may photocopy the design and use the copy; though, your spell will be more powerful if you draw the symbol yourself. Set your doll on top of the symbol and concentrate on the person you are targeting. Chant the following nine times:

Damballah, may I [your name]
come out victorious in dealing with [the person's name].

Anoint the doll with Damballah Wedo oil. Keep in a box lined with Spanish moss and set the box on top of the ritual symbol. Repeat the ritual as often as necessary until the desired results are achieved.

Ancient Chaldean Spell

This spell is based on ancient Chaldean magic. Create an effigy in the image of your enemy out of wood, fabric, or other burnable material. Take some nails and drive them into the effigy while chanting the following:

I forge this image, I bewitch it,
the malevolent aspect, the evil eye,
the malevolent mouth, the malevolent tongue,
the malevolent lip, the finest sorcery,
Spirit of the heavens, conjure it! Spirit of the earth, conjure it!

Burn the effigy and spread the ashes in the yard of the one you wish to dominate.

Whiskey Doll to Keep a Man from Wandering

This is a spell from Harry Middleton Hyatt's *Hoodoo Conjure Witchcraft Rootwork.*[58] It is a spell designed to control a man and keep him from wandering around. The original transcription of the interview follows my translation of the spell.

Make a small doll baby to represent the man you want to keep at home. Stick the doll baby in a wide-mouth mason jar or equivalent, and pour a bottle of whiskey into the jar. Add some sugar and a bit of your own urine. Close the jar tightly and wrap it in a cloth and set it in a corner of your bedroom. Leave for seven days. It is said your man will return within those seven days.

Like many of the spells Hyatt recorded, there are no specific directions for what to do after the seven days. I suggest burying the jar in the front yard, a common practice for these types of works in hoodoo.

Original transcription (comments in brackets are Hyatt's):

1842. Dis whiskey an' sugah—fo' a man if he's runnin' round. Yo' cut dat yet-tah domestia—ah mention dat, an' yo' cut chew a little man out. Dat's right in de shape of a little man an' put it in dat bottle.

[What bottle?]

In de bottle whut chew put dat whiskey in, yore whiskey an' yore chamber lye an' de sugah. An' take dat an' set it back, if yo' want him tuh stay dere; an' set it in a cloth in a corner, jes' let it set down jes' lak de man do an' let it stay dere

---

58. H. M. Hyatt, *Hoodoo-Conjuration-Witchcraft-Rootwork, Memoirs of the Alma Egan Hyatt Foundation,* 1974.

seven days. An' if he's out anywhere in town, he'll come back. But yo' got'a have de shape of de man altogethah.

[He doesn't drink that whiskey or anything? Just keep it in the bottle?]

No suh—dat's all. [Memphis, Tenn., (1548), 2813:1.]

SIXTEEN

Spells for Protection, Countermagic & Defense

Why can't we just live in peace? Alas, as long as there is envy, jealousy, and hatred in this world, we are at risk of being under attack. There are people who just thrive on in misery and conflict, and there are people who will always covet that which you have.

This section includes Voodoo dolls, conjure dolls, and doll babies that can be used either by themselves or with spells for protection, countermagic, and defense. These dolls will help protect you against the evil eye, avert negative energy, block and reverse black magick, thwart psychic vampirism, guard the home from evil, give protection from helpful spirits, and reflect negativity back to its source.

The dolls and spells in this section can be performed at any time; however, there are certain correspondences that may enhance your work. It is commonly believed among occult practitioners that the best times for works of protection and defense are Tuesdays and Thursdays under a waxing moon or full moon.

Chango Spell for Protection

In the Yoruba tradition, Chango is a mighty warrior, the orisha of thunder and lightning. He carries a double-headed axe and dresses in satin and tiger skin. When you hear the roaring of thunder, it is Chango riding his white horse and looking to serve justice.[59]

In this tradition, dolls are used as representations of the various orishas and kept on altars or in special vessels. For this spell you will create a doll to represent Chango.

Create your Chango doll during a thunderstorm. Collect some water from the storm and hand wash some red and white fabric in it. Allow to air dry.

While the fabric dries, wash a thunderstone in red wine.

Once the fabric is dry, insert a piece of lightning struck wood in the doll along with a magnet. Write the following on a piece of virgin parchment:

Forgive me Lord, for I have sinned
In the mountains, the fierce wild female animal can be found
With a sprinkling of Holy water, my troubles are overcome
I implore you, Chango, the Mighty King, to conquer my enemies
Chango, protect my house and all those around me
In the mountains, the fierce wild female animal can be found
With a sprinkling of Holy water, my tormentors are overcome
I implore you, Chango, the Mighty King, to conquer my enemies
Chango, protect my house and all those around me
Protect me, the person who is making this prayer, from witches and magic and
  wicked men
Lord, I am a spark of the sun and you have seen the value of lifting up your axe here.
I want you to take each of my enemies away from me
Lord I am a spark of the sun and you have seen the value of lifting up your axe here
I want you to take each of my enemies away from me and punish them and
  bring them defeated to my place
As you are my lord Jesus Christ at the foot of the holy cross
In the name of the Father, the Son and the Holy spirit amen.

Light a white candle. Place the doll in front of the candle and the thunderstone to the left of the candle. Sprinkle some holy water on the doll and the thunderstone, and then sprinkle both with gold magnetic sand. Read the petition aloud. Offer

---

59. See http://agolaroye.com/Chango.php for more information about Chango and the orishas. See also D. Alvarado, *A Guide to Serving the Seven African Powers*, 2009.

Chango a bowl of cooked cornmeal, some okra, and a glass of red wine. Tell him these are for him in return for his protection. When you are done, fold the paper three times towards you and tuck it inside the doll. Sew the doll closed. Your petition is now sealed. Allow the candle to burn down, and dispose of the food in the woods somewhere under a tree. Put the candle wax remains in a paper bag and leave at a crossroads. Keep your Chango safe in a wooden box when you are not working with him.

Fiery Wall of Protection Voodoo Doll Spell

This spell is a variation of a traditional New Orleans hoodoo spell. Perform this spell to remove an enemy from your home or workplace, or anywhere you frequent and do not want your enemy to frequent as well. For this spell you will need the following items:

7 purple offertory candles
1 white offertory candle
Fiery Wall of Protection oil
Fiery Wall of Protection sachet powder
Graveyard dirt
Fireproof dinner plate
Cross
Angelica root
Clean white cloth
Black Voodoo doll
St. Michael the Archangel holy card

Lay the cross in front of the plate and anoint with the Fiery Wall of Protection oil (see page 23 for formula). Dress the Angelica root with the Fiery Wall of Protection oil as well. Lay a circle of protection around the cross and Angelica root with the Fiery Wall of Protection sachet powder. As you are dressing the cross and the Angelica root, repeat the following:

Saint Michael the Archangel, protect me and defend me in battle.

When you are done preparing the cross and Angelica root, lay the St. Michael the Archangel holy card in the center of the circle and sprinkle with a little Fiery Wall of Protection powder. Place the white candle in the circle. Then, take the seven purple offertory candles and inscribe on them the names of seven people, angels, saints, or spirits who represent your personal army of protection—one name per candle. Anoint the candles with the Fiery Wall of Protection oil and roll in the sachet powder. Set the candles on the circle of protection around the cross, Angelica root, and St. Michael the Archangel holy card. Sprinkle a bit more of the Fiery Wall of Protection sachet powder on the St. Michael the Archangel holy card, cross, and Angelica root.

Place the graveyard dirt in a fireproof dinner plate. Attach a photo of your target to the Voodoo doll with a black pin and/or write your target's name nine times on a piece of parchment paper. On top of and crossing the person's name, write nine power words that describe your feelings for this person, such as *wicked, evil, hate, sick*, and so on. Attach the name paper to the doll with a black pin. Lay the doll on the graveyard dirt in the plate. Place the doll in the plate to the left of the circle. Do not put the doll and plate inside your circle of protection.

Begin lighting the purple candles going clockwise. Light the white candle next. The repeat the following prayer:

> *Saint Michael the Archangel, defend me in battle.*
> *Be my protection against the wickedness and snares of the devil.*
> *May God rebuke him, I humbly pray;*
> *and do Thou, O Prince of the Heavenly Host—*
> *by the Divine Power of God—*
> *cast into hell, Satan and all the evil spirits,*
> *who roam throughout the world seeking the ruin of souls. Amen.*

Now, speak a heartfelt prayer of your own, asking your spiritual army led by St. Michael the Archangel for protection and Divine assistance with the expulsion of your enemy. Light the black Voodoo doll on fire. As it burns, say:

> *Your evil is returned!*
> *Your evil is undone!*

Your evil is done!
You are done!

Let the doll burn out in the fireproof dish. When it is extinguished, place the plate with the graveyard dirt and the remains of the doll in a paper bag.

Take the cross, Angelica root, and St. Michael the Archangel holy card and wrap in the clean white cloth. Anoint with Fiery Wall of Protection oil and sprinkle with Fiery Wall of Protection powder. Tie it closed with seven knots to represent your Divine Army of Seven. Hang it behind your front door for protection. You can also carry it with you as a protection talisman.

Take the paper bag with the remains of the black Voodoo doll, the plate, and the graveyard dirt and go to one of the forty-two Cities of the Dead (New Orleans cemeteries). Find a tomb with a cross and throw the wrapped dish with the doll and graveyard dirt as hard as you can against the wall of the tomb, breaking the plate. Turn around and leave the cemetery and never return to that spot.

If you do not live in New Orleans, you can go to any cemetery and find any grave with a cross to use to finalize this spell.

Spell for Victory over Evil

This spell is to be performed as a defense against enemies and those who cause drama and chaos in your life. Make a black Voodoo doll and name it with the name of your enemy. Anoint daily with Victory over Evil oil. Repeat for nine days and burn a white candle each day. On the ninth day, take the remains of the candle wax and the Voodoo doll, place it in a paper bag, and leave at a crossroads.

High John the Conqueror Protection Spell

One of the most well-known hoodoo curios is High John the Conqueror root. The subject of many blues songs and the main ingredient in many mojo bags, High John the Conqueror root is believed to be an effective talisman in and of itself for power, prosperity, mastery, good luck, and protection. Indeed, it is a powerful mechanism of protection against being hoodooed.

But just who was John the Conqueror? According to legend, he was a spirit that came across the ocean with the enslaved Africans. He is said to have accompanied them to offer hope and a sense of humor. As the story goes, he would take the form of a slave and outwit the master with any number of crazy antics. It was he who stood up to "Massa" when others couldn't. He played the role of trickster in many ways, going against the grain, never being punished and always getting a laugh. Once the slaves were free, he took up residence in the root of a plant that could be carried to bring protection and good luck to whoever needed it.[60]

For this spell, you will create a brown conjure doll while burning a white candle. Get the largest whole John the Conqueror root you can find (make sure it is a nice round whole root as it represents his manhood). Stuff the doll baby with cedar, Spanish moss, a lodestone, magnetic sand, and nine pieces of Devil's Shoestring root. Place the High John root down near the doll's private area and sew the conjure doll closed. Baptize your doll baby in the name of Johnny the Conqueror.

To baptize your doll baby, you will need some holy water or holy anointing oil. Repeat the following words, replacing [name] with the name of your doll, and using the name of your personal Higher Power as appropriate. Repeat the following:

> *I baptize thee* [name], *in the name of the Father, Son, and Holy Ghost* [you may substitute your personal Higher Power here]. *In life, this is now who I wish you to be. With the highest blessings of our most High Lord. So be it.*

Sprinkle a little holy water on the doll, and the baptism is complete.[61]

To use your Johnny the Conqueror doll baby, simply anoint him with High John the Conqueror oil and hold him close to your heart. Then, repeat "John over John" like a mantra. Get a rhythm going so that it takes you into a mesmerized state and you are completely focused on your need and your goal. That's it—that's all that is needed to gain courage, protection, and luck in money matters or love. Repeat as often as needed.

---

60. Haskins, *Voodoo & Hoodoo.*
61. See my 2009 book, *Voodoo Dolls in Magick and Ritual,* for a discussion of Voodoo doll baptism and consecration.

The natives of Old Calabar used periodically to rid their town of the devils which infested it by luring the unwary demons into a number of lamentable scarecrows, which they afterwards flung into the river.

Confuse an Enemy

This spell is particularly effective to counteract persistent spiritual attack. Make a black, brown, or grey doll baby and stuff it full of Spanish moss. Add thirteen pieces of Devil's Shoestring (this will trip up your attacker) and thirteen dead spiders with their fangs intact. Lay your doll on a piece of wood. Name the doll for your enemy and tell it you are stopping them from further attack. Then, nail thirteen small nails into each limb, fastening the doll to the board. The doll should be securely nailed to the board. With a pair of sharp scissors, cut off the doll's head. Bury the board with the doll's body face down near a garbage dump. Bury the head far away from the rest of the doll to completely confuse your enemy and prevent him from being able to take any further action against you. As long as the doll is nailed to the board and its head and body are separated, your enemy will be powerless against you.

Spell to Stop Evil

by Doktor Snake

If someone is persistently casting evils spells on you, the following ritual will stop the black work in its tracks. This is what you do: Using clay, create a small doll resembling the person casting evil spells on you. Tie a piece of string around the doll's neck and let the doll set for four hours.

Now, bake the doll in an oven, which will lead to the doll being "strangled" by the string. Take the doll out of the oven and let it cool. Place a few drops of Van Van oil on the figure and hide it in a safe place, away from prying eyes.

This will return any evil spells done on you and will give the evildoer a metaphysical "kick" to keep them in line.

Formula for Van Van Oil

Palmarosa essential oil
Lemon verbena essential oil
Lemongrass essential oil
Vetivert essential oil
Citronella essential oil
Ginger grass essential oil
Geranium essential oil

Blend equal parts of the above ingredients in a base of almond oil to which a small amount of vitamin E has been added as a preservative.

Simple Spell for Protection

Create a Voodoo doll and baptize it in the name of St. Michael the Archangel. Attach a St. Michael talisman or medal to the doll and anoint daily with St. Michael oil while asking St. Michael for his unfailing protection. Light a seven-day Hoodoo candle with a picture of St. Michael on it while praying and anointing your doll.

Spell for Protection against Evil Spells

This spell uses the magickal properties of the Angelica herb as its main power ingredient. Angelica, also known as archangel and masterwort, is an herb that has medicinal properties, culinary uses, and magickal properties. According to the *Master Book of Herbalism* by Paul Beryl,[62] Angelica is considered one of the most valuable herbs of protection. For its use with Voodoo dolls, we shall concentrate on the protective properties of this herb.

Angelica is associated with the Archangel Michael. One explanation for the name of the herb is that it comes into bloom near his feast day and is connected to the Christian observance of the Annunciation.[63] Because of this, all parts of the

---

62. P. Beryl, *Master Book of Herbalism* (Blaine, WA: Phoenix Publishing,1984).
63. "Avicenna: Quality Herbal Essences," http://www.avicennaherbs.co.uk/cgi-bin/avicenna/page.cgi?p=aw.

plant are extremely effective against evil spirits and malevolent sorcery. Angelica is believed to be of such importance that it became known as the Root of the Holy Ghost.

To make a Voodoo doll that will function to protect you from evil spells or break an existing hex, create a poppet doll of blue fabric on one side and gold fabric on the other. Stuff it with the Angelica herb, along with some rosemary, chamomile, and cinnamon. Add one piece each of tiger eye, turquoise, and lapis lazuli stones, as well as the resins myrrh, frankincense, and copal. Anoint with Fiery Wall of Protection oil. Sew the doll closed. Cut out a photo of Archangel Michael and fix it to the face of the doll.

Hold the doll between your throat and solar plexus and focus intently on stopping the evil that has befallen you. Visualize the Archangel Michael rescuing you with his sacred sword. Pray with all of your heart by speaking these words:

> *Michael, protect me.*
> *Michael, give me the strength to face this situation and my enemies with*
>   *courage.*
> *Michael, cut away all evil and falseness with your sword so that I may be free*
>   *to be myself and live a life of peace and harmony.*
> *Michael, your powerful sword is a living flame that will cut away all of my*
>   *fear and restore me with strength and power.*
> *Michael, I believe you are here to help me, to protect me, and to break any curse*
>   *that may have been placed upon me.*
> *Archangel Michael, I know you will clear the road to happiness and safety for*
>   *me and my family.*
> *Thank you for hearing my prayer.*

You may reuse this doll as many times as you like to repeat this spell. Keep the doll next to the entrance of your home so that it may function as the guardian and protector for you and your family.

Neutralize Enemy Attacks

This poppet is designed to neutralize the power of those who intend to harm you or your family, either by slander, evil eye, black magick, or emotional and physical harm. Create a poppet out of purple fabric. Sew the edges of the doll closed except for one side. Be sure to leave a rather large opening. Stuff the doll with blessed salt (salt that has been prayed over with the Psalm 23), orris root, frankincense, myrrh, and rue. On a piece of parchment paper, write the following:

I neutralize the power of [name your enemy] *to do me any harm. I ask that this be correct and for the good of all. So mote it be.*

Roll up the parchment, tie it with black thread to bind it, and place it inside the doll. Sew the poppet up so as to seal in its contents. Then, light a white candle and carefully allow the candle wax to drip on the edges of the poppet while turning the poppet counter-clockwise. This is to completely seal the contents inside. Finally, bury the poppet in your front yard in a secret place where it will not be disturbed by humans or animals. If it is dug up and the contents spill out, the protective charm will be broken.

CONJURE DOLL SLAVE NARRATIVE

Clara Walker, an ex-bondwoman in Arkansas, told of a black "witchdoctor" who punished a slaveholder by creating "a little man out of mud" in his image, and then sticking a thorn into the back of the doll. "Sure 'nuff, his master go down with a misery in his back," she claimed. "An de witchdoctor let de thorn stay. . . until he thought his master got 'nuff punishment. When he took it out, his master got better."[64]

64. Y. Chireau, *Black Magic: Religion and the African American Conjuring Tradition* (Berkeley: University of California Press, 2006).

Sanctus Spiritus Gris Gris Doll for Protection against Evil Spirits and All Manner of Witchcraft

Burn a white candle while creating a Voodoo doll out of white muslin or cotton fabric. Before you sew the doll together, write the following on the front of the doll with a fabric pen (see figure 22 on next page):

I.

N. I. R.

I.

SANCTUS SPIRITUS.

I.

N. I. R.

I.

All this be guarded here in time, and there in eternity. Amen.

You must write all the above on the fabric. Then, stuff the doll with cotton and protective herbs such as eucalyptus, basil, mint, and sage. Add other protective items such as cat's eye shell, graveyard dirt, and black hen feathers. You can use up to thirteen items and only an odd number of ingredients. Anoint the doll with Fiery Wall of Protection oil. Then, sew the doll up. Keep the doll in a safe place in your home for ongoing protection. The characters or letters signify: "God bless me here in time, and there eternally."

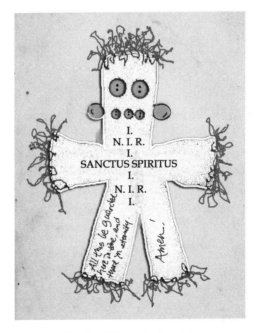

Sanctus Spiritus Voodoo doll.

Voodoo Doll Spell for Protection against Betrayal and Bewitchment, and to Be Blessed Always

This spell should be performed on Holy Thursday (referred to as Maundy Thursday in medieval times), the Christian feast or holy day falling on the Thursday before Easter that commemorates the Last Supper of Jesus Christ with the Apostles.

Set up an altar with seven white candles. While burning the candles, sit before your altar and create a Voodoo doll that is white on one side and red on the other. Inside the doll, place a silver dime and a dollar. Add some sage, chamomile, mint, rosemary, and myrrh. Sew the doll closed. Write as a petition on blank parchment paper the following prayer:

> *Like unto the cup and the wine, and the holy supper, which our dear Lord Jesus Christ gave unto his dear disciples on Maundy Thursday, may the Lord Jesus guard me in daytime, and at night, that no dog may bite me, no wild beast tear me to pieces, no tree fall on me, no water rise against me, no fire-arms injure me, no weapons, no steel, no iron, cut me, no fire burn me, no false sentence fall upon me, no false tongue injure me, no rogue enrage me, and that no fiends, no witchcraft and enchantment can harm me. Amen.*

Attach the prayer paper to the doll with a white pin and keep the doll on your altar before the candles. After a time of quiet contemplation, put out the candles. Repeat the ritual by relighting the candles and reciting the prayer out loud every day until Easter Sunday. On Easter Monday, clear everything off of your altar except the Voodoo doll. Take the candle remains to a crossroads or running stream of water and discard there. To enhance the protective value of this ritual, donate some food or money to the poor after you discard the ritual remains. You may keep the doll wrapped in white cloth in a safe place and repeat the ritual every year.

The Germans made the Mandrakes into dolls, dressing them with care and respect, and keeping them in caskets.

Paper Voodoo Doll Protection Spell

Cut a Voodoo doll out of white paper similar to the one in figure 34. Write the following words on the paper doll:

Ananiah, Azariah, and Misael, blessed be the Lord, for he has redeemed us from hell, and has saved us from death, and he has redeemed us out of the fiery furnace, and has preserved us even in the midst of the fire; in the same manner may it please him the Lord that there be no fire.

I.
N. I. R.
I.

Fold the paper doll up, being careful to fold the prayer of protection towards you. Carry the protective talisman with you at all times and nothing evil can touch you.

Voodoo Doll for Defense against All Evil

by Doktor Snake

If you feel you are under threat from curses and jinxes, this Voodoo doll spell will defend you against all evil. If a bad worker is on your case, nothing they throw at you will touch you. You will be invulnerable.

This is what you do: Write your name on a piece of parchment paper (thick art paper is fine). Attach this to a pink Voodoo doll, which you can make or buy, using pink cotton or thread. Anoint two brown Drive Away candles with Uncrossing oil and also sprinkle some on the doll.

Now anoint two purple Satan Be Gone candles with Jinx Removing oil, and again, sprinkle some on the doll.

Place the four candles on the floor to form a square. Lay the doll in the center. Light the four candles and walk around them four times. As you circle the candles, whisper the following Voodoo success chant four times:

Eh! Eh! Bomba, Hen! Hen!
Canga Cafio Te

Canga Mouna Dele
Canga Dahi La
Canga Li.

Leave the Voodoo doll in the square overnight. The next morning, wrap the doll in a pink cloth and put it in a drawer or cabinet near a window. Don't let anyone else see it. Repeat the ritual as necessary.[65]

Carolina Dean's Basic Protection Spell

To work this spell, you will need:

A doll made in your own likeness
A clean white handkerchief
Spring water
Kosher salt

First, take a clean white handkerchief and soak it in spring water to which you have added half a cup of kosher salt. Let the handkerchief soak in this salted water overnight during a full moon.

The following day, gently ring out the handkerchief and place it outside where it will dry in the clean air and sunshine. When the handkerchief is completely dry, take a doll baby that represents you and wrap it in this handkerchief. Place the handkerchief-wrapped doll in a safe place.

If you choose, you can enhance this ritual by lighting candles and incense, chanting, reciting prayers, and so on . . . but this is not required. Symbolically, you have surrounded yourself with a "white light" of protection; in more practical terms, however, the residual salt left in the handkerchief will act as a shield against any spells, hexes, or jinxes thrown in your direction.

---

65. Find more Voodoo doll spells at Doktor Snake's website: http://www.doktorsnake.com.

Voodoo Poppet Spell to Stop Gossip

Make a Voodoo poppet out of black cloth and stuff it with moss. Name the doll the name of your enemy. For example, you can say something like "Your name is Howard and I have made you. As I have made you, so shall you cease to speak ill of me." Continue to say this as if it were a chant until you complete the doll. Make two eyes out of buttons and stitch the mouth closed.

Spell to Silence Gossip

Create a meat poppet out of ground pork that has been mixed with black pepper, horseradish, rue, yarrow, and valerian. As you are shaping the meat and herbs into a human figure, tell it to shut up and be quiet, and to stop telling stories and spreading rumors. Stick the doll in the oven and cook it until it is well done and you can't see any pink in the meat. Dispose of the doll by burying it in a cemetery far away from your home, leaving it out in the sun to spoil, or giving it to some dogs to eat.

Shut Yo' Mouth Poppet Spell

Create a poppet out of brown fabric and stuff with Spanish moss. Sew three X's for the mouth. As you sew each X, say:

Shut yo' mouth
Shut yo' mouth
Shut yo' mouth
By the power of 3 so mote it be

Take the doll to a cemetery and nail it to a tree. Cover its mouth with a piece of duct tape and leave it.

Spells to Deal with Thieves

If you have ever been ripped off, you may want to exact revenge against the perpetrator. Being ripped off is one of my biggest pet peeves. I get really irked when someone steals from me. In fact, it taps into my personal power in such a way that I pity the fool who has ripped me off.

Let me put it into perspective for you. People who know me will tell you I am a generous person. In fact, my generosity can be to my detriment at times, but that's a whole different issue. My point is, if you want something of mine so badly that you would steal from me, just ask me and I will probably give it to you, or help you get what you need (within reason of course . . . I am only a mortal and I am not independently wealthy . . . yet).

So, here are a couple of pretty darn effective spells for catching thieves.

A Doll to Trip Up Thieves

by Carolina Dean

This is a conjure doll spell contributed by Carolina Dean. It's a little doll made for business owners who have had problems with thieves, robbers, and shoplifters. It can be used in your home as well to protect your dwelling from the same.

To begin, simply make yourself a doll baby by cutting out two human-shaped pieces of cloth. Sew them together and stuff the doll with cotton bunting, peat moss, and so on. In addition to the stuffing you use, include the following items:

Dried red peppers
Vandal root
Black pepper
Salt
Devil's Shoestring

I usually place a whole dried red pepper down each leg near the foot to hot-foot the criminal away. The Vandal root is used partly because "vandal" is another word for someone who willfully destroys your property, but it also keeps out unwanted visitors (thieves, criminals, robbers). The salt has the duel task of protecting your home/business and keeping unwanted visitors from coming back. Black pepper also has a reputation for preventing unwanted visitors. Finally, the Devil's Shoestring will cause them to "trip up" and make a mistake that will get them caught.

As you place each item inside the doll, speak to its spirit, asking it to perform its specific function and to work with the other herbs and minerals. If you wish, you can write a petition on a piece of paper and place this inside the doll as well. This could be something as simple as "This doll represents any person that would enter my home (or business) to rob or steal from me." When you have completed the doll, smoke it in incense to bring it to life and assign it its task.

Take the doll and hang it upside down from a piece of string by one leg over the front entrance to your home or business. Each time you successfully catch a shoplifter, avert a robbery, or catch a thief, take a pin and stick it in the doll to ensure that the charges are successfully "pinned" on the thief. [66]

Carolina Dean doll to trip up thieves.

Cause Male or Female Thieves to Be Frozen in Time

This spell is adapted from a remedy by John George Hohman's *Pow Wows; or, Long Lost Friend.* To make a thief stand still so that they can be caught, create a purple doll for commanding, domination, and power. Stuff the doll with some fern to prevent further thieving, as well as dirt dauber nest and tobacco for power and domination. Name the doll if you know the name of the thief in question, or name the doll "the thief who stole. . . ." Pick up your doll and tell it you are taking it for its last walk. Walk around and repeat the following three times:

---

66. Visit Carolina Dean's website, www.carolinaconjure.com, for many more spells.

*Oh, Peter, oh Peter, borrow the power from God; what I shall bind with the
bands of a Christian hand, shall be bound; all male and female thieves, be they
great or small, young or old, shall be spell-bound, by the power of God, and not
be able to walk forward or backward until I see them with my eyes, and give
them leave with my tongue, except it be that they count for me all the stones
that may be between heaven and earth, all rain-drops, all the leaves and all
the grasses in the world. This I pray for the repentance of my enemies.*

Pray the Apostle's Creed and the Lord's Prayer. It is believed that if not released
from this spell before the sun shines again, the guilty party or parties will die. You
can release them by saying one of two things: "In the name of St. John, leave," or
"The words which have bound thee shall give thee free."

Apostle's Creed

I believe in God, the Father almighty, creator of heaven and earth.
I believe in Jesus Christ, his only Son, our Lord.
He was conceived by the power of the Holy Spirit and born of the Virgin
    Mary.
He suffered under Pontius Pilate, was crucified, died, and was buried.
He descended into hell. On the third day he rose again.
He ascended into heaven and is seated at the right hand of the Father.
He will come again to judge the living and the dead.
I believe in the Holy Spirit,
the holy Catholic Church, the communion of saints,
the forgiveness of sins,
the resurrection of the body,
and life everlasting.
Amen.

The Lord's Prayer

Our Father, who art in heaven,
Hallowed be thy Name.
Thy kingdom come.
Thy will be done,
On earth as it is in heaven.
Give us this day our daily bread.
And forgive us our trespasses,
As we forgive those who trespass against us.
And lead us not into temptation,
But deliver us from evil.
(For thine is the kingdom,
and the power, and the glory,
for ever and ever.)
Amen.

Custom Voodoo doll made in the likeness of a particular person.

SEVENTEEN

SPELLS FOR SELF-IMPROVEMENT

All of the spells in this section are designed to improve your quality of life in a variety of ways. Each of the works involves creating a doll that represents you, so be sure to add some personal effects such as hair, fingernail clippings, or a piece of clothing that you have worn. In this way you create a sympathetic link from the doll to you, and whatever is done to the doll will also be done to you. It goes without saying that you should be sure to always protect these kinds of dolls so that they don't fall into the wrong hands.

Blessed Unbinding Voodoo Doll Ritual

This spell is designed to help you free yourself of ideas and experiences that keep you guilt-ridden or stuck. It involves creating a Voodoo doll that will be a representation of yourself and then binding the doll. The binding is symbolic of the ties that bind you.

Create a Voodoo doll out of white fabric and stuff with cotton batting. Take a rope and tie it around the body of the doll. Start winding it around as if to bind the doll. Each time you wind the rope, say: "This is for my insecurities [you fill in the blank here]." Wind again and call out another experience, belief, or idea that keeps you stuck. Keep winding in this fashion until you run out of rope. Then, take the bound Voodoo doll and place it in front of a white candle. Just before bedtime, recite the Lord's Prayer backwards and untie the doll. Burn the rope in the flame of the candle and when it is burned, say: *I am bound no more. So Be It.*

An Egyptian Memory Spell

Take a piece of tin foil and engrave it with the Sacred Eye of Horus after sunset (see figure on next page). Pour some milk into a clean glass and place the tin foil under it. Make twelve dolls out of Egyptian barley bread in the shape of female figures. Say the following formula three times and eat the barley bread dolls on an empty stomach, and you will know the Power.

> *BORKA BORKA PHRIX PHRIX RIX O'...*
> *ACHACH AMIXAG OUCH THIP LAI LAI LAMLAI LAI LAM MAIL*
> *AAAAAAAA IIIY E'I AI O'O'O'O'O'O'O' MOUMOU O'YIO' NAK NAK*
> *NAX LAINLIMM LAILAM AEDA ... LAILAM AE'O O'AE' O'AE'*
> *E'OA' AO'E' E'O'A O'E'A, enter, Master, into my Mind, and*
> *grant me Memory, MMM E'E'E' MTHPH!*

Do this monthly, facing the moon, on the first day of the month. Prostrate yourself before the Goddess [i.e., Selene, the moon], and keep the foil Eye of Horus as an amulet.[67]

Recipe for Egyptian Barley Bread[68]

2¼ teaspoons yeast
½ cup lukewarm water
2 tablespoons honey
½ teaspoon salt
1 egg, lightly beaten

---

67. *The Greek Magical Papyri in Translation, Including the Demotic Spells,* Volume 1, Hans Dieter Betz, Ed. (Chicago: University of Chicago Press).
68. Adapted from H. Mariana, *Breads of the World* (New York: Berkley, 1955).

2 tablespoons shortening
2 cups barley flour

Combine yeast, water, and honey, and let proof five minutes. Add salt, eggs, and shortening. Stir in flour and blend until dough is workable. Turn out onto a lightly floured surface and knead for a couple of minutes. Place in a large greased bowl, turning to coat. Cover with a towel and let stand in a warm place for ninety minutes. The dough will rise slightly, but will *not* double. Turn the dough out onto a lightly floured surface and knead again. Shape into twelve female forms about one-half inch thick. Place on a lightly greased baking sheet. Cover with a towel and let rest for one hour.

Preheat oven to 425°F. Bake 15-20 minutes, or until bread is pale brown and sounds hollow when tapped. Cool on a rack.

Sacred Eye of Horus.

Make Me Irresistible

You can't get any easier than this spell. Make a pink poppet and stuff with lavender, rose petals, a magnet, and red clover. Attach a St. Valentine medal to the doll and anoint daily with Fire of Passion oil while stating: "I am irresistible. No one can resist me. I am magnetic. All that I want will be drawn to me." Repeat as often as needed.

Spell for Restraining Anger

This spell is adapted from the Papyri Graecae Magicae. If you want someone to cease being angry with you, make a conjure doll and stuff with myrrh. Write this name of anger on the doll: "CHNEO'M" [probably Egyptian Khnum]. Hold the doll in your left hand and say: "I am restraining the anger of all, especially of him, NN, which is CHNEO'M."[69]

Año Viejo Ecuadorian New Year's Poppet

In researching doll magic traditions in other cultures, I identified several countries that involve entire communities in ceremonies, which use life-size or larger effigies of human figures to represent something specific. The Ecuadorian annual ritual burning of the "Año Viejo" is one such communal celebration that I thought appropriate for this book.

The burning of the Año Viejo is a tradition well known in several Latin American countries, including Ecuador, Colombia, and Venezuela, but it is said to be found all through Latin America from Mexico to Uruguay. Most certainly each region has its own variations of the ritual, but the general purpose is the same—destruction of the old to make way for the new.

The tradition uses fire to symbolically burn up past regrets, mistakes, resentments, and frustrations of the old year in order to usher in the hopes, dreams, and aspirations of the new one. In Ecuador, each year on the thirty-first of December people create large dolls to represent the "old year" or year's end. These comical creations are constructed out of old clothes—often pieces of clothing from each family member—and are made in the likeness of a particular family member. The chosen family member writes a humorous will that states all the things they are leaving behind and to whom they are leaving them and places the mock will on their own front door. Alternatively, a handwritten note explaining why it must be burned is pinned to the doll.

The dolls are stuffed with a variety of materials such as paper, sawdust and straw, and even fireworks and Chinese rockets to ensure that old bad habits and regrets go out with a bang. Hosiery is sometimes used for the construction of arms and legs. Wooden sticks are placed down the backs of the dolls so they can sit or stand upright, and the dolls are placed in funny poses: as if riding a bike or sitting on the side of a building like a drunkard with a beer in hand.

---

69. *The Greek Magical Papyri in Translation, Including the Demotic Spells*, Volume 1, Hans Dieter Betz, Ed. (Chicago: University of Chicago Press).

In some regions of the country such as the Andes, elaborate masks made from paper maché in the likeness of a family member are placed on the doll. In other regions, these masks represent more archetypal or worldly figures such as politicians, artists, athletes, and superheroes. Sometimes, they are made to represent community undesirables—people who folks would rather see disappear for the greater good.

At midnight, the dolls are burned as a ritual of purification and renewal, a cleansing of old, negative energy, individual and collective failures, regrets, bad habits, bad luck, and evil from the previous year. The burning of the dolls signifies the transition of the old year into the New Year through the purifying power of fire. Often, the dolls are heaped together in big piles to create large fires in the middle of the streets. It is said that jumping over the burning dolls brings good luck to those who successfully accomplish this feat. Dinner and celebration typically follow the ritual burning.

The origin of the Año Viejo ritual is unclear. Some suggest that its roots lie in pagan Roman and pre-Roman traditions that were brought to many Latin American countries during colonial times. Others surmise that the tradition stems from a yellow fever epidemic that necessitated the mass burning of corpses in the streets.

The Año Viejo tradition can be easily adapted to a more personal level in a ritual that can be performed with a small doll for the purpose or cleansing and renewal, or even as an Enemy Be Gone-type of Voodoo spell. To create your own Año Viejo doll, make a poppet from a piece of your clothing if the doll is to represent you or the clothing of another if it is to represent another person. Stuff it with straw, cedar shavings, and a page from a newspaper of the year that is passing (or even from a year in which something bad happened that you wish to target and erase). A simple Google search can help you find newspapers from specific dates that you can print out and use. Write on a piece of paper that which you wish to leave behind or change and either pin it to the doll or place it inside the doll before you sew it closed. Read your statement before attaching it to the doll, and then at midnight on the thirty-first of December, burn the doll and watch your regrets go up in smoke.[70]

---

70. S. Hardy, "An Ecuadoriuan Tradition, the New Year's Burning of the Año Viejo Dummies Clears the Slate for a Better 2013," http://www.cuencahighlife.com/post/2013/12/27/Ecuadorian-tradition-the-New-Years-Eve-burning-of-the-dummy-clears-the-slate-for-2009.aspx.

EIGHTEEN

WISHING SPELLS

Wishing Doll Spell for Luck, Health, and Protection

The wishing doll for good luck, health, and protection against evil uses the Cross of Caravaca as its source of power. It is said that all wishes, no matter how extravagant, are granted when the cross is used in combination with the appropriate prayers.

Create a Voodoo doll in white and attach a Cross of Caravaca to the heart region. You can buy a Cross of Caravaca at any botanica and in many online curio shops (see the section of recommended suppliers at the end of this book). If you cannot find one, then draw one or photocopy a photo of one and attach it to your Voodoo doll with a white pin. Nail the doll to the inside of the door to your home or to the wall at your place of business for good luck and protection. It can also be hung from a baby's crib to protect it from the evil eye. When you are sick, remove the doll from the wall and place over the affected part of your body and pray each of the following three times: Glory Be, to the Passion of Jesus Christ, Hail Mary to the Holy Virgin. Pray one Our Father to Saint Benito. When you are finished praying, kiss the doll and hang it back on the door or wall. When you have a wish, take the doll and hold it with both hands. Close your eyes and visualize your wish as if it were true. Recite another round of the prayers as described above. Take the doll and hold it to your heart for a moment, and then kiss it and hang it back on your door or wall. Repeat this ritual daily to show your devotion until your wish is granted.

Seven Wishes Voodoo Doll Love Spell

This spell is most effective when performed during a new moon or full moon. Make a red doll baby and stuff with red clover, seven Job's tears, and a piece of rose quartz. Using Dove's Blood ink, write a petition with seven things you desire for the relationship you wish for. You can use the back of the petition if you run out of room. Fold the petition twice, each time folding the paper towards you. Pin the petition to the doll in the heart area with a red pin.

Every day for three days, hold your doll close to your heart and visualize you and your lover together. On the third day, burn the petition in the flame of a red candle and scatter the ashes in the direction of your lover. Wrap your Voodoo doll along with the talisman in a red cloth and keep somewhere safe in your bedroom.

Wishing Fetish

Cut a piece of leather and make a doll of it. In this, place thirteen pennies, nine cotton seeds, seven Job's tears, and a bit of hair from a black hog. Rub the doll while making a wish to make that wish come true.

San Simón Wish-Granting Doll

San Simón, also known as Maximón (pronounced *masheemon*), is a folk saint venerated in various forms by Mayan people of western Guatemala. San Simón is referred to as "Champion of the Hopeless" by some folks because of his ability and willingness to work with just about anyone for just about anything. He is able to grant wishes of any kind, if you offer him the right gifts.

San Simón is believed to be a Catholicized form of the pre-Colombian Mayan god Mam (meaning *ancient one*). There are many, many forms of San Simón, his evolution coinciding with the influence of European explorers and missionaries.[71] Under the influence of Catholicism, he became associated with Judas. According to another theory, he is the deification of one of my ancient ancestors, Pedro de Alvarado. Pedro de Alvarado was a Spanish conquistador who was responsible for bringing Catholicism to the indigenous people. He married the daughter of the Aztec king Xicotencotl el Viejo and was responsible for having the first Mixtec children in the Americas.

As the incarnation of the ancient Mayan god of sexuality, San Simón is said to have slept with all of the wives in a village one day while the men were out in the fields. When they returned and discovered what he had done, they were so pissed off that they cut off his arms and legs! This story explains why effigies of San Simón are short and stubby with no arms.

Altars to San Simón always have a doll or effigy that represents him, along with cloth that is characteristic of the indigenous peoples of South and Central America. People turn to him with requests of good health, family harmony, job security, good crops, and the like. He has what is referred to as a dark side as well, but I like to refer to it as human. He is said to grant requests that have something to do with revenge and success at the expense of others.

In areas where San Simón is venerated, he resides in a different house each year, moving to a new residence on the first day of November. He is tended to by two people referred to as *Cofradia,* who take care of him and maintain his altar. He is typically dressed in eighteenth-century garb, reportedly an attempt by the indigenous people to convince the Christians of their successful conversion (not!). He usually has a lit cigarette or cigar in his mouth and wears a black cowboy hat. In some places, he wears dark sunglasses and a bandana. He often has a hole in his mouth in which a drink is poured. The alcohol passes through a tube and into a vessel and is reused at a later time.

For this ritual, I will describe how to petition San Simón for a wish. First, you must create an effigy of him, or you can buy a statue if you prefer. I think there is something to be said for creating your own effigy because it will be personal and full of your own energy, not some store's or manufacturer's, and who knows how many other people may have touched a store-bought figure or statue. To create a

---

71. See Pieper's 2002 book, *Guatemalan Folk Saints,* for a fabulous and detailed description of San Simón and his evolution throughout history.

San Simón doll, find a thick tree branch or tree stump (not so large that you can't carry it) and carve out a hole in the top. You will be placing some items inside the hole so your San Simón is not empty. Since no one really knows what goes inside San Simón (except for the initiated), we will use items known to be sacred to his tradition. Fill the hole in the stump with rose petals, forty red beans, forty black beans, pine resin, and Indian tobacco. Seal the hole by placing another small stump on top of his body. This will function as his head. If making him out of a stump is beyond your ability, then simply create a doll out of fabric and stuff with the aforementioned items. You will also need Guatemalan fabric and numerous color-ful scarves to dress him. If you are really crafty, you can mold a face for him out of clay or paper maché, or carve his face in the stump. Otherwise, you can buy one of those unfinished full face masks available at any craft store, and paint it. Purchase a small black cowboy hat to keep on his head. These little hats can be found at any craft store.

Next, create a special place for San Simón. He should be kept in a corner of the bedroom, preferably on the floor, along with a glass of water, a red candle, corn tortillas, incense (copal), and flowers. You can add textiles from Latin America and folk art pieces to further decorate his altar space. You may also offer him cigars, cig-arettes, coins from several countries, hot sauce, parrot feathers, stones, and aguardi-ente. Incense should be burned daily at noon sharp, and an offering be made in the name of the person needing help.

Depending on the nature of your wish, you should use candles in colors that are appropriate. In his tradition, the colors are as follows:

Red: Love, faith, and good will

Green: Prosperity and help in business

Blue: Luck and work

Pink: Health, hope, purity, innocence

Yellow: Protection of loved ones

Black: Counteract evil and negativity, against enemies, dispel spiritual attacks

White: *Protection for children*

Once you have his space set up and the correct color of candle to go with your wish, write down your petition on a piece of paper and set it under the candle. Then, tap on the glass of water three times and say the following prayer:

> *Oh powerful San Simón, help me with all of my actions and with any dangers that may arise that I may need assistance. If I need help in matters of love, you will draw the one I love closer to me, if it be business, that I will be successful, if it be enemies, that you will help me to overcome them, and to keep hidden troubles away from me. I offer you your cigar, your tortilla, your liquor, and your candles if in return you will keep me safe from any danger I may come across.* [State your petition.] *Amen.*[72]

It is customary to keep his altar set up and work with him daily for best results.

---

72. Prayer is found on the back of seven-day San Simón candles, reproduced in Pieper's 2002 book, *Guatemalan Folk Saints.*

NINETEEN

JAPANESE VOODOO SPELLS

Japanese Voodoo? Who knew? *Ushi no Koku Mairi*, commonly called *Japanese Voodoo*, is the practice of cursing with straw dolls (wara ningyo), a tradition that dates back to the Kofun period (250–538 CE). *Ushi no Koku Mairi* literally means "Going to the shrine at the time of the Ox at two o'clock in the morning."[73] To anyone familiar with the Japanese tradition, going to the shrine at two o'clock in the morning usually means someone is up to no good. For most people, the thought of going to a shrine in the dead of night during a full moon is scary enough, but going equipped with a straw doll, a hammer, and long iron spikes called *gosunkugi* makes the thought even scarier.

In more ways than one, Ushi no Koku Mairi rituals are surprisingly similar to Western rituals using Voodoo dolls. For example, the Japanese straw doll can be used for a variety of purposes, just like a Voodoo doll. In fact, one need not have a straw doll and may substitute a photograph or even a paper doll with the target's name written on it. Working with the doll is the same. You can make a person fall in love with you by binding the doll with a rope. You can curse an enemy by nailing

---

73. S. Levenstein, "Straw Voodoo Doll Kit: Nail the Boss at Home," http://inventorspot.com/articles/straw_voodoo_doll_kit_nail_boss_home_31716.

the doll to a tree or shrine gate and piercing it with a stick for seven days in a row. You can use it for protection from diseases by tying the doll to a tree and hitting a nail through its chest. Heck, you can even beat the devil out of it if you are so inclined. *Oni*—ferocious Japanese demons with tiger skins that have long claws and horns on their heads—are said to fly around looking for the souls of evil people. To avoid an encounter with that nightmare, one only needs to perform a ritual with a straw doll for seven days during a full moon at two o'clock in the morning, and then place the doll in the northeast part of the home for protection.

The lore associated with this kind of Japanese image magic has endured for centuries and continues to persist in the 21st century. Aggressive marketing campaigns advertising Ushi no Koku Mairi kits that contain a straw doll, a hammer, a couple of candles, and fifteen-centimeter-long nails are targeted to the young Japanese demographic. The tradition has moved into the Internet, garnering the dubious distinction of being the focus of countless anime episodes, online games, and videos that promote cyber cursing via virtual Voodoo dolls. These games explain the tradition and further its international reach. The dolls in these games now take on different forms—iron doll, cotton doll, mist doll, and light doll—all having special magic spells with which to defeat an enemy. Once a subject of folklore, Ushi no Koku Mairi is now a myth reanimated through the use of the Internet and modern technology, giving anyone the ability to cast curses without having to go anywhere at two o'clock in the morning (except to the virtual shrine that is now the computer).

Interestingly, it is against the law in Japan to actually perform Ushi no Koku Mairi. This suggests that it is a tradition that is taken very seriously and that its consequences are most dire.

Modern bastardizations aside, the ancient Japanese doll curse is the ultimate *get back at yo' ex* revenge ritual. We only need to recount the origin of the ritual to see the truth in that statement. As the legend goes, around the year 800 a beautiful young woman went to the Kibune shrine in Kyoto and cursed her husband in a seven-day-long ritual for cheating on her. From there, her story became legend and the tradition was born. While nailing the doll, you pray to the Kami spirits to curse the person. According to Chinese cosmology, the northeast direction is believed to be bad luck because it is the direction whence demons come. Therefore, for the best results, the doll should be facing northeast.

Adapting this longstanding tradition to modern times is not difficult. However, one should think long and hard before performing it as it is said that the end result is the ultimate destruction and death of the victim. This is how I propose it could be done by anyone foolish enough to try it.

Japanese Cursing Doll

This ritual will be performed for seven days in a row, so be sure to set up in a private place where you won't be disturbed. Performing the ritual in secrecy is of the utmost importance, for it is said that if anyone sees a person performing the ritual or otherwise finds out, the ritual will backfire. According to the tradition, the only way to prevent this unfortunate consequence is to kill the eyewitness.

For this ritual you will need:

A straw or paper doll
3 white candles
Personal effects from the target (hair, fingernail clippings, piece of clothing, photograph, and so on)
Hammer
7 long nails
Raffia (optional)
Board or piece of wood from a powerful tree like an oak or ash tree, but preferably a piece of cedar wood
White face paint
Knife
Mirror
Wooden comb
Loose-fitting white clothes and a sash or belt

Barring access to a shrine that contains a sacred tree housing ancient Kami spirits, you are going to create your own shrine where you will perform the ritual. To keep as much of the tradition as possible, perform this ritual only during the hour of the ox between one o'clock and three o'clock in the morning during a full moon. Just as Western tradition states that the three o'clock hour is when the veil between the worlds of the visible and the invisible is the thinnest, the hour of the ox is the traditional witching hour in Japan. The Japanese believe this is the time when evil spirits such as the Yurei and Yokai make their presence known.

Be sure to dress in white for this ritual. Paint your face white, even though using the color white may seem counterintuitive when viewed from a Western perspective (actually, from a magical perspective, the color white can be used for any work because it is considered a neutral color that may be imbued with any type of energy the practitioner desires). In the Japanese tradition, however, the manner of dress is as important as the ritual and, in fact, is part of the ritual. It is said that how a person dresses is a reflection of their intention. Some say that one must dress like the demon one needs to become to perform the ritual (another version of the ritual has the practitioner paint their face red). Others say that one must dress in a manner that will most effectively summon the evil entity that will torment and ultimately destroy the victim. Variations in dress correspond to variations in rituals. For this version, dressing in white and wearing white is believed to make you look like a ghost. For this ritual, I suggest you summon a demon rather than becoming one.

Place the knife in your belt and hang the mirror over your neck so that it covers your chest. The knife is purely symbolic and *I am not recommending you kill anyone*. The mirror and knife are for the practitioner's spiritual protection. You should be barefoot for this ritual.

The wooden comb is to hold between your teeth to keep you silent while performing the ritual. Again, this is different from Western magical methods where incantations are spoken when summoning demons. Here, it is all mental.

Set up your altar so that it is facing northeast. Light two white candles and set them about two feet apart on your altar. Light the third candle and place it at the top and between the other two so that you have a triangle formation. Here, I am taking the liberty of having you set the candles on the altar instead of on your head since most people will not have access to the correct head crown in which to place the candles. However, if you want to put them on your head, knock yourself out. (Note that a company selling these dolls has a similar ritual where the person performing the spell lights a single candle on an altar or table and ties the doll to a round piece of cedar wood, then nails the doll once in the mouth for the first day.) Place a board that is at least two inches deep, twelve inches wide, and fourteen inches long between the candles. Take the personal effects of the target and attach them to the doll with pins by wrapping them around the doll (in the case of a piece of clothing) or by placing them inside the doll. If you place the personal effects inside the doll, wrap the doll securely using plain raffia to make sure the items stay inside.

Now, lay the doll onto the board, face up. Each day, for seven days, you are to dress as directed above when you approach your altar. Drive one nail into the doll on each day. Silently pray to the Kami to assist you in seeking revenge. On the last day, drive the last nail through the doll's head.

It is believed that the most vengeful spirit will come forth, equaling the anger you project. So if you feel any remorse or sadness or pity for your victim, the curse will not work.

Japanese Teratu Bōzu Dolls

Japanese *Teratu Bōzu* (meaning sunshine monk) dolls are traditional, handmade magickal dolls used as amulets or talismans to bring about good weather.

This is an interesting custom. Like the simple ghosts made by children in the United States for Halloween, with white tissue paper or cloth tied with string and hung from trees and whatnot, the Japanese Teratu Bōzu dolls are made from white tissue paper or cloth that is tied with string and hung from the eaves of the front porch. However, these Japanese figures are not meant to represent ghosts at all. Rather, they are wishes for better weather often made by children who want to go outside and play.

Beneath the custom is a fascinating bit of cultural lore. Aside from being wishes for better weather, they were originally made as prayers to ancient Chinese gods and to one in particular, Hiyoribo, a Yokai from Japan's monster clan. Hiyoribo is said to live in the mountains and to come down during the summertime to bring sunny weather. If it is rainy or overcast, he is not present.

Nowadays, Teratu Bōzu dolls are considered talismans that bring good weather. Sometimes, though, they are used by farmers to bring the opposite—rain. In this case, the figures are hung upside down, head first, and are called "furefure bozu or ameame bozu (both meaning roughly *the rain monk*) or ruterute bozu, which is simply teruteru bozu said backwards."[74]

---

74. Z. Davisson, "What Are the Teratu Bozu?," http://hyakumonogatari.com/category/magical-dolls/; N. Miyata, "Weather Watching and Emperorship," *Current Anthropology* 28:4 (1987): 13-18.

A folksong or nursery rhyme is recited while the dolls are hung. This is the English translation:

Teru-teru-bozu, teru bozu
Do make tomorrow a sunny day
Like the sky in a dream sometime
If it's sunny I'll give you a golden bell
Teru-teru-bozu, teru bozu
Do make tomorrow a sunny day
If you make my wish come true
We'll drink lots of sweet rice wine
Teru-teru-bozu, teru bozu
Do make tomorrow a sunny day
But if the clouds are crying (it's raining)
Then I shall snip your head off

Instead of the folk song, sometimes just the following is said when the dolls are hung: "Fine weather priest, let the weather be good tomorrow."

If the dolls are successful, faces may be drawn on them. Then, they are taken down and their heads are washed with sake. Finally, they are tossed in a river, sometimes along with offerings of cups of sake. While this practice is reminiscent of common disposal methods of ritual remains in hoodoo, there is an important difference. The Japanese believe that rivers are connected to the gods and the afterlife. Thus, the figures are not "disposed of" as they may appear to be; rather, they are made as offerings to the river spirits.

If you are in need of good weather, make yourself one of these figures from childhood and put your own wishes into it. Then hang it from your front porch, tree, or in the window as a lucky talisman.

TWENTY

GOETIC RITUALS

Who doesn't want a genie in a magic lamp? Objects that are imbued with supernatural powers or possessed by spirit forces are the stuff of legends. Generally speaking, the priest or conjurer creates the object and calls forth a spirit to reside in that object. The manner in which this is done varies according to tradition and purpose. In this section, a technique based on principles of ceremonial magick for calling forth an entity to reside in a magickal doll is described.

Spirits that are called forth to serve those that summon them go by many names. Referred to as *servitors,* they are beings that are created by conscious thought and intention using specific techniques of evocation. In Haitian Vodou, they may be referred to as djabs: personal spirits with specific magickal functions. In the Western esoteric tradition, such entities may be referred to as *thought forms*; in Arabic magic they are *djinns*; and in Tibetan magic, they may be called *tulpas*. Servitors can be usefully deployed to perform a wide range of tasks or functions on your behalf. Servitors can be created to work with one particular situation or event or they can be created with a specific expertise in one area, such as healing.

The rituals that follow are based on evocational principles of the Goetic magic and necromancy traditions and are for advanced magicians. As such, they should not be attempted by anyone who lacks the necessary training in ritual magick.[75]

Magickal Doll for Invoking Spirits

Take a cleansing spiritual bath prior to conducting this ritual. If you do not do this, you may conjure up something that is less than desirable. A spiritual cleansing bath can consist of a cup of blessed sea salt added to warm bath water during which you pour the water over your head seven times. Allow yourself to air dry before proceeding. You can prepare blessed salt by praying Psalm 23 over it prior to use.

Now, create an altar or sacred work space. You may add a statue of the deity of your choice, and on either side set a candlestick with seven candles, your doll (yet to be created), and an incense burner or censor in the middle. Most important is that you are in a space where you will not be disturbed.

There are four basic concepts to consider before creating a magickal doll to house a personal spirit. First, you must decide on the general intent of the spirit you wish to call forth. For example, determine the area of your life you need to influence. Health? Wealth? Love? Once this is decided, you can decide which symbols and magickal correspondences to use in creating your doll. According to Franz Bardon in *The Practice of Magical Evocation,* if you want to summon a planetary entity, you should use the following colors and associations:

Beings of Saturn: *Dark violet*

Beings of Jupiter: *Blue*

Beings of Mars: *Purple*

Beings of the sun: *Yellow, gold, or white*

Beings of Venus: *Green*

---

75. Franz Bardon, *Initiation into Hermetics: A Course of Instruction of Magic Theory and Practice* (Wuppertal, Germany: Dieter Ruggeberg, 1987).

Beings of Mercury: *Opalescent, orange*

Beings of the moon: *Silver, white*

The idea here is to use the color that corresponds to the purpose and work that the conjurer wishes to accomplish to create the doll. According to Bardon, beings associated with the planets will only manifest if the right color and environments are provided. Should you desire an elemental being, consider the guidelines provided by Bardon:

> *Thus, when working with beings of the elements for the fire spirits the lamp will have to have ruby-red glass or accordingly coloured that the lamp radiates a red light. For spirits of the air or the so-called fairies, a dark blue light is necessary. The lamp therefore has to be covered with dark-blue cellophane paper or with a piece of silk of that colour, thus creating a blue light. Water-spirits or so-called water nymphs must have a green light. For spirits of the earth a yellow colour which may have a shade of brown will have to be used. The Akasha-colour can be used as a universal light, in which case the lamp must have a violet colour. High spirits or intelligences from the world beyond the planets need a white light.*[76]

In the practice of ceremonial magic, this is important for identifying the nature of the beings evoked.

Once the purpose and color are decided upon, the next step is to identify a talismanic seal to use as the foundation for creating your magickal doll. See pp. 182–3 for some examples of seals of power that are appropriate for this work. Experienced magicians may create their own seals through intense concentration and meditation. Many use the Pentacle of Solomon (figure 20) for such purposes.

On a piece of parchment paper, draw the seal or talisman that represents the ultimate symbol of power to you. When you have chosen or created the seal that corresponds with the purpose of your work, you should consecrate it by smoking it with incense and running your finger over it while focusing on its purpose.

---

76. Bardon, *Initiation into Hermetics.*

Lay the talisman down on your altar and begin creating your magickal doll over the talisman. Create the doll in the color appropriate to your purpose and create a robe for it in the same color. Next, create a belt out of the same fabric. To create a robe, cut out a piece of fabric that is twice as long as the doll and one inch shorter than the width. Fold the fabric in half lengthwise and again widthwise, and snip the corner to make an opening in the middle of the fabric. Open up the fabric and slip it over the head of the doll.

Cinch the waist with the belt and attach a lion charm to the center of the belt. The lion charm represents power and dominance. Slip a gold chain around the doll's neck. The chain connects the doll to all great magicians—past, present, and future. Do not let anyone touch this doll, as it must not be contaminated with anyone's energy other than your own. Lay the doll down on top of the seal.

Make a copy of the same seal and attach to the chest of the doll's robe. If you are especially artistic and skilled at sewing, you can embroider the design onto the robe.

The next order of business is to bless your work area. You can do this by using incense that corresponds to the type of spirit you will be evoking. Below are the types of incenses that are associated with the various beings (adapted for our purposes from Bardon's *The Practice of Magical Evocation*):

Earth: Sage and elder pith in equal parts and in pulverized state

Moon: Aloeswood and benzoin, each in pulverized state to which a pinch of camphor is added

Mercury: Mastic; alternately, create a supercharged mixture of equal parts mastic, carnation blossoms, aniseed, juniper wood, chamomile blossoms, and valerian roots, everything in pulverized state

Venus: Cinnamon; alternately, create a supercharged mixture of cinnamon, rose blossoms, coriander seed, lily blossoms; all in equal quantities and pulverized state

Sun: Sandalwood; alternately, create a supercharged blend of equal parts sandalwood powder, myrrh, aloeswood powder, saffron, carnation blossoms, laurel leaves, each in pulverized state

***Mars:** Onion seeds; alternately, create a supercharged blend of equal parts seeds of onions, leaves of stinging nettles, grains of mustard seed, hemp seeds, rue leaves and peppermint leaves; all in pulverized form*

***Jupiter:** Saffron; alternately, create a supercharged blend of equal parts saffron, linseed, violet roots, peony blossoms, betony leaves, and birch leaves; each in pulverized state*

***Saturn:** Pulverized black poppy seeds; alternately, create a supercharged blend of equal parts black poppy seeds, willow leaves, rue leaves, fern, cumin, and fennel seeds*

For anything else, a universal incense blend is recommended: myrrh, storax, benzoin, and aloeswood (pulverized and in equal quantities).

Now, you must focus all of your attention to the being you wish to evoke. You must become one with the Divine and with the planetary sphere in which you are working. You must concentrate on the characteristics of the being and visualize it coming forth.

If you have prepared your space and your doll correctly, and you are focusing your attention sufficiently, you should hear the voice of the being in your mind. Once you hear its voice, you may call out to it, first in your mind and then out loud. You should hear it again. At this point, hold your hands open and facing each other about six inches above your magickal doll. You are calling the spirit through your hands and into the doll. Call it by name, if you know its name. If you do not know its name, name it. Tell it to pass through the portal you are providing with your hands and into the vessel you have carefully prepared for it.

You should now be able to see the spirit taking residence in your doll. You will know if this has occurred. Once you are certain your spirit has successfully entered your doll, you can talk to it and tell it what you want and need from it. If it is agreeable, it will help you. Sometimes, the spirit may impart specific knowledge to you, or ask for an offering. You should give it what it wants if the request is reasonable. If not, you should release it and try again with a more suitable thoughtform.

Whenever you are finished interacting with your being, you must release it back to the sphere from which it came. Sometimes the being will prefer to stay and reside in the doll. However, it must be its choice to do so and not yours. This ritual is not meant to be a form of spiritual slavery.

If you have been successful and the spirit has been agreeable, then you will be able to call it forth at will by repeating the ritual, intensely focusing and visualizing it in your mind's eye and directing it into your doll.

The "Seal of Solomon" or "Pentacle of Solomon" as given in the 17th-century grimoire The Lesser Key of Solomon.

Seal of the Spirit of Fire from the Seventh Book of Moses.
Use this seal to obtain power, popularity, influence, and obedience.
Place beneath a red Voodoo doll anointed with Ylang Ylang oil
while burning a red candle.

THE VOODOO DOLL SPELLBOOK

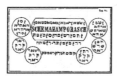

Seal of white and black magic from the Seventh
Book of Moses. Use this seal to compel spirits to appear
and to serve your needs. Place beneath a white Voodoo doll
anointed with St. Jude oil while burning a white candle.

Solomon's seal, also known as the Interlaced Triangle,
is an ancient talisman that has been used in every religion. It is
considered all-powerful, being the perfect sign of the Absolute. As a
whole it stands for the three virtues love, truth, and wisdom.

Chinese characters for power, strength, and force.

Reiki symbol of power.

Keys can represent power because they symbolize the
unlocking of infinite wisdom and opportunity.

The Elder Futhark is the oldest form of the runic alphabet, used by
Germanic tribes for Proto-Norse and other migration-period Germanic
dialects of the 2nd to 8th centuries for inscriptions on artifacts
(jewelry, amulets, tools, weapons) and runestones. This is the rune is
called Uruz, and represents strength and power.

Magickal Doll to Raise the Ghost of a Loved One

This spell is for the purpose of calling forth the spirit of a loved one of your choice and takes place over a period of nine days. It is an advanced spell and should not be performed by a novice.

The number nine has special significance in the occult and is based on the Law of Three. The Law of Three states that all petitions should be done in triplicate. According to Malbrough, the first time you state your petition, you are making your conscious mind aware of your intentions. The second repetition awakens the rational mind. The third repetition brings you into full contact with spirit. Finally, when a prayer, request, or intention is repeated nine times, it is said it will be heard by God.[77]

For this spell you will need to gather some personal effects of your target. Hair, fingernail clippings, articles of clothing, and photographs are particularly effective. The idea is to use anything that contains a lasting impression of your target. Then, you will need to decide on a date on which to perform the ritual. It must be a date that will always be remembered by the soul of the person, such as a birth date or anniversary. Then, you will carefully prepare a doll from clean white cloth. The doll can be a poppet or a sticks and moss doll. Insert the personal effects inside the doll and attach a photo of your loved one on the front of the doll with a red pin.

Prepare a "room" for the doll that resembles the house or home of your target. This will serve as your altar. Surround the doll with flowers and change them out daily so they are always fresh. Place a clean white cloth next to the doll that will serve as a veil. Place a wine glass or chalice on the altar. For the next nine days, you must refrain from engaging in sex and other intimate physical contact with anyone.

Every evening at the same hour, enter the room with the light of one candle. On the first night, sit in front of the altar you have created and place the candle behind you. Stay seated in front of the doll in absolute silence for one hour. During this hour you should be focusing all of your energy on manifesting the spirit by visualizing life with this person exactly as you remember it. When the hour is complete, smudge or fumigate the room with white sage, being sure to get all four corners of the room. Place the veil over the doll and back your way out of the room when you are finished.

---

77. R. Malbrough, *Charms, Spells & Formulas* (St. Paul, MN: Llewellyn, 2012).

In the mornings, dress as if you are going out on the town with your loved one. Prepare a meal of fresh fruit and bread and bring it into your doll's room. Unveil the doll. Spread out a white cloth in front of the altar and place the food on the cloth. Take some of each food item and place them on the altar as an offering to your desired one. Put the food on a special plate just for the one you are invoking. Pour some wine into the glass or chalice. Pour yourself some wine. Now, you must eat and drink everything you have brought in, so make sure to bring only as much as you can eat. Clear everything away except the wine and a piece of bread that you place directly in front of the doll.

On the second evening, enter the room again with a single candle. Do not unveil the doll. This time you will light a small fire in a cauldron or chiminea in front of the altar. Bring some loose resin incense such as myrrh or copal. Place some of the incense on the fire nine times, each time calling out the name of the person you are invoking. Blow out the candle and allow the fire to burn out. When the fire is reduced to ashes, place some more incense on the embers and pray to the deity that your loved one served. You must pray as if you were that person, and identify yourself by the name of that person. Put yourself in the mindset of your loved one as much as is possible. Speak as if you are one and the same.

Stand before the altar quietly for thirteen minutes. Then start to speak to your magickal doll as if it contains the soul of your loved one. Speak as if your loved one is in the room with you. Beg him or her to come to you. Shout their name three times and fall to your knees with both hands over your face. Call out their name three more times, this time in a soft, loving tone of voice. Slowly open your eyes and observe for manifestations. Repeat this ritual for seven more days.

On the ninth day, unveil the magickal doll and repeat the ritual for a final time. The one you invoke should manifest before you.

TWENTY-ONE

A LITTLE LAGNIAPPE

Lagniappe is a Louisiana French term for "a little something extra." It is customary in New Orleans to throw in a little something extra when selling something or whenever the mood strikes. I like to think of it as a hallmark of Southern hospitality. So in that spirit, here are a few lagniappe spells and lore for you that didn't seem to belong in any of the other categories. Enjoy!

Voodoo Doll Spell to Keep Your Cat or Dog from Wandering Off

Anyone who has ever had a pet dog or a cat knows the possibility of their animal companions wandering off. To keep your dog or cat close to home, create a poppet in the form of a cat if you have a cat, or a dog if you have a dog and fill it with sweet herbs such as rosemary and clover to keep your pet drawn to you, sage to protect them, and cedar to control them. Procure some hairs from your pet and place them inside as well. Sew up the doll and attach some good luck charms to the outside, such as a four-leaf clover, a lucky horseshoe, a cross, or a holy medal of St. Francis of Assisi. Anoint the poppet with Holy oil (or pure olive oil if you don't have any Holy oil) and pray the following prayer:

> *Blessed are you, Lord God,*
> *maker of all living creatures.*
> *maker of all living creatures.*
> *On the fifth and sixth days of creation,*
> *On the fifth and sixth days of creation,*
> *you called forth fish in the sea,*
> *you called forth fish in the sea,*
> *birds in the air and animals on the land.*
> *birds in the air and animals on the land.*
> *You inspired St. Francis to call all animals*
> *You inspired St. Francis to call all animals*
> *his brothers and sisters.*
> *his brothers and sisters.*
> *We ask you to bless this animal.*
> *We ask you to bless this animal.*
> *By the power of your love,*
> *By the power of your love,*
> *enable it to live according to your plan.*
> *enable it to live according to your plan.*
> *May we always praise you*
> *May we always praise you*
> *for all your beauty in creation.*
> *for all your beauty in creation.*
> *Blessed are you, Lord our God, in all your creatures! Amen.*

If your pet is sick, pray the following:

> *Heavenly Father,*
> *you created all things for your glory*
> *you created all things for your glory*
> *and made us stewards of this creature.*
> *and made us stewards of this creature.*

THE VOODOO DOLL SPELLBOOK

If it is your will, restore it to health and strength.
If it is your will, restore it to health and strength.
Blessed are you, Lord God,
Blessed are you, Lord God,
and holy is your name for ever and ever. Amen.

Finally, put a chain around your pet poppet and attach it to the front door or place it somewhere behind the front door. Just make sure it is attached to your home in some fashion.

St. Francis of Assisi's Protection Doll for Pets

The relationship between humans and their pets is like no other because communication is at its most basic. The unconditional love and undying loyalty are virtues few people can achieve, yet they are second nature to many animals.

In the Roman Catholic tradition, people will take their pets to church with them for a special blessing. At Franciscan churches, a friar with brown robe and white cord often welcomes each animal with a special prayer.

There may be occasions when you want to bless your animal companions or provide them with extra protection. When this is the case, make the following Voodoo poppet and perform the St. Francis of Assisi blessing to keep them safe and blessed.

Make a poppet in the likeness of your pet. For example, if you have a dog, make a dog poppet; if you have a cat, make a cat poppet; if you have a bird, make a bird poppet; and so on. Stuff the poppet with a blend of the following herbs: mugwort, sage, cedar, Dragon's Blood, and lavender. Add some of your pet's hair, feathers, nails, scales, etc. and a piece of paper bearing their name to the doll and stitch it closed.

Place the poppet on your altar and say the following prayer in remembrance of St. Francis of Assisi's love for all creatures.

Franciscan Blessing for All Animals

Blessed are you, Lord God,
maker of all living creatures.

On the fifth and sixth days of creation,
you called forth fish in the sea,
birds in the air and animals on the land.
You inspired St. Francis to call all animals
his brothers and sisters.
We ask you to bless this animal.
By the power of your love,
enable it to live according to your plan.
May we always praise you
for all your beauty in creation.
Blessed are you, Lord our God, in all your creatures! Amen.

Franciscan Blessing for a Sick Animal

Heavenly Father,
you created all things for your glory
and made us stewards of this creature.
If it is your will, restore it to health and strength.
Blessed are you, Lord God,
and holy is your name for ever and ever. Amen.

As the prayer is offered, the poppet is gently sprinkled with holy water. When you are done, keep the doll in a safe place in your home.

How to Render Oneself Invisible

The following magickal doll spell comes from the Greater Key of Solomon. In the month of January in the day and hour of Saturn, make a small image of yellow wax in the form of a man. Write with a needle above the crown of its head and upon its skull the following character:

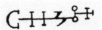

Afterwards, write upon a small strip of the skin of a frog, toad, or parchment the following words and characters:

hets, hets, hets, ✢ ✣ ✝ A ⌐⌐

Hang the doll using one of your hairs from the ceiling at the midnight hour, and burning incense under it, say:

METATRON, MELEKH, BEROTH, NOTH, VENIBBETH, MACH,
and all ye, I conjure thee O Figure of wax, by the Living God, that by the vir-
tue of these Characters and words, thou render me invisible, wherever I may
bear thee with me. Amen.

After having burned incense again under it, bury it in the same place in a small box, and every time that you wish to pass or enter into any place without being seen, you shall say these words, with the waxen doll in your left pocket:

Come unto me and never quit me whithersoever I shall go.

Afterwards, take the doll carefully back to the before-mentioned place and cover it with earth until you need it again.

Voodoo Doll Spell to Find a Missing Person

This spell comes from the tradition of the Holy Death (Santa Muerte) practiced in Mexico and recently in the United States.

Santa Muerte, also known as *Señora de las Sombras* ("Lady of the Shadows"), *Señora de la Noche (*"Lady of the Night"*), Señora Blanca* ("White Lady"), *Señora Negra* ("Black Lady"), *Niña Santa* ("Holy Girl"), and *La Flaca* ("the Skinny One"), is a great example of the syncretization of Catholicism and Mesoamerican spiritual traditions. In Mesoamerican cultures, death has always been venerated. This is evident in the popular celebration of the Day of the Dead. The spiritual tradition of Santa Muerte, however, has been practiced mostly in privacy until recently, though it remains condemned by the Catholic Church in Mexico.

Santa Muerte is depicted as a skeletal figure wearing a long white robe and holding a scythe and a globe. There is a wide variation in images among followers, but the skeletal figure is standard. Unlike the Day of the Dead, this tradition has not been embraced by the masses. When it first became known outside of the privacy of individual homes, images of Santa Muerte were burned. People were vehemently against it.

Working with Santa Muerte is similar to working with any of the saints or loas. She is petitioned for favors of all kinds, though she is believed to have the power of performing miracles. She can make someone fall in love with you or cause someone to die for you if it is justified. Like Pomba Gira, when invoked as Lady of the Night, she has the power to protect prostitutes and those who work in the shadows and in dangerous nighttime positions. She keeps these people safe from violence and protects them from attack.

Santa Muerte's feast day is November 1st or August 15th. On this day, she is dressed as a bride.

If you have a loved one who is missing, has disappeared or run away, been kidnapped, or whom you cannot find for any reason, try petitioning Santa Muerte for assistance. For this spell you will need:

Photo of the missing person
Personal item belonging to the missing person (hair from a hair brush, a letter, etc.)
Personal items belonging to family members
Image of the Holy Death
Piece of clothing or other fabric belonging to the missing person
Long piece of thin white lace

Take the photo of the missing person and on the back of it write the person's name. Below this, write the name of the family members who are looking for the person.

Make a doll out of a piece of clothing or fabric belonging to the missing person. Insert several personal items belonging to the missing person and their family members inside the doll and sew it shut. Attach the photo of the missing person along with the image of Santa Muerte to the doll by wrapping it with the white lace. Tie one knot in the lace and say the Holy Death prayer. Do this for nine nights in a row, tying one knot per night. Keep the doll close to you until your loved one is found.

THE VOODOO DOLL SPELLBOOK

Holy Death Prayer

Miraculous and Majestic Holy Death:
I ask that with your immense power, you locate my loved one (state the name of the missing person) *and bring them back to me safely. Free them of all malevolence and danger, guide them safely home where they belong. We rejoice eternally in all the glorious power that God has granted you. This is why, my protector and master, I ask that you concede this great favor, grant this great miracle that I ask for in this prayer. Amen.*

[Say three Hail Marys and three Our Fathers]

The Magic Maiden

By Frances Jenkins Olcott

In a huge chamber sat four-and-twenty Ladies around a banquet table, all in splendid robes as though for a wedding. At the head of the table sat the Lady, Kiisiki's Mother, on a golden chair.

Elsa did not know what to look at first, everything around her was so magnificent and glittering. Upon the table stood thirteen dishes on gold and silver salvers. One dish alone remained untouched, and was carried away without its cover being lifted. Elsa ate all kinds of costly foods, which tasted better than sweet cakes. The four-and-twenty Ladies talked in low tones, and Elsa could not understand what they said.

Then the Lady, Kiisiki's Mother, spoke a few words to the maid who stood behind her chair. The maid hurried out and returned with a Little Old Man whose beard was longer than himself. He made a bow, and stood by the door. The Lady pointed a finger at Elsa, saying:

"Look carefully at this peasant child. I am going to adopt her. Make me an image of her, which tomorrow may be sent instead of her to her village."

The Old Man looked sharply at Elsa. Then he bowed and left the room.

After dinner, the kindly Lady said to Elsa, "Kiisiki has begged me to let her have you for a playmate. Is it really true that you wish to stay?"

Elsa fell on her knees, and kissed the Lady's feet and hands. But the Lady lifted her up, stroked her head and tear-stained cheeks, and said:

"If you will remain a good and diligent child, I shall care for you till you grow up. No misfortune shall touch you, and you shall learn with Kiisiki the finest handwork and other things."

Just then the Little Old Man came back carrying a trough of clay on his shoulder, and a little covered basket in his left hand. He set the clay and the basket on the floor, took a bit of the clay and shaped it into a doll. The Lady examined the doll on all sides, then said:

"Now we need one drop of the Maiden's own blood."

Elsa, when she heard these words, turned pale from fright. She was sure that she was about to sell her soul to the Evil One. But the Lady comforted her by saying:

"Fear nothing! We do not want your drop of blood for anything bad, only for your own future happiness."

Then she took a gold needle, stuck it into Elsa's arm, and gave it to the Little Old Man. He thrust the needle into the doll's heart. After that he laid the doll in the little basket to grow, and promised to show it to the Lady the next day.

Then they all went to rest. Elsa found herself on a soft bed in a sleeping-chamber.

The next morning, when she woke in the silk-covered bed with soft pillows, she opened her eyes and saw rich clothes lying on a chair nearby. At the same moment a maid stepped into the room, and bade her bathe herself and comb her hair. Then the maid clad her in the beautiful clothes. Her peasant clothes had been taken away during the night. What for? Now you shall hear!

Her own clothes had been put on the clay doll, which was to be sent to the village in her stead. During the night, the doll had grown bigger and bigger, till it was the very image of Elsa. It ran about like a human being. Elsa was frightened when she saw the doll so like herself, but the Lady, noticing her terror, said:

"Fear nothing! This clay doll cannot hurt you. We are going to send it to your parents. The wicked woman may beat it all she wishes, for the clay doll can feel no pain."

So the clay image was sent to her parents.[78]

---

78. F. J. Olcott, *Wonder Tales from Baltic Wizards* (London: Longman's, Green & Company, 1928).

RESOURCES

The following websites carry many of the supplies, ingredients, and background information related to the spells contained in this book.

Creole Moon
www.creolemoon.com
info@creolemoon.com
This website is owned and operated by the author, Denise Alvarado. Creole Moon's Spiritual Art for Sacred Spaces: Publications, Magickal Apothecary and Spiritual Art for Cultural Preservation carries a unique selection of hand-crafted, artisan-made, superior quality products for worship, ceremony, and devotion for alternative faiths.

Doktor Snake's Voodoo Spells and Conjure Shack
www.doktorsnake.com
drsnake@doktorsnake.com
Doktor Snake is a legendary cult author, hoodoo bluesman, and Voodoo spellcaster. His books include *Doktor Snake's Voodoo Spellbook* and *Mary Jane's Hash Brownies.*

He provides high-quality spellcasting services and old-time hoodoo card readings to clients around the world.

Carolina Conjure
www.carolinaconjure.com
Online *Book of Shadows,* created by Carolina Dean to share his beliefs, practices, and experiences as a practitioner of Wicca and folk magick.

Medicines and Curios

www.medicinesandcurios.com
Witchcraft supplies, Wiccan supplies, gothic and occult supplies. Providing magickal, ceremonial, spiritual, ritual items since 1965.

BIBLIOGRAPHY

Alvarado, Denise. *The Voodoo Hoodoo Spellbook*. Charleston: Create Space, 2009. "Banish, Bind, and Enemy Be Gone: The Anatomy of the Voodoo Curse." http://www.squidoo.com/voodoocurses.

Beckwith, C. "The African Roots of Voodoo." *National Geographic* 188 (1995), 102-113.

Betz, H.D., ed. *The Greek Magical Papyri in Translation Including the Demotic Spells*. Chicago: 1986.

Bodin, R. *Voodoo Past and Present*. Lafayette, LA: University of Southwestern Louisiana, 1990.

Budge, E. A. W. *Egyptian Magic Late Keeper of the Egyptian and Assyrian Antiquities in the British Museum*. London: Kegan, Paul, Trench and Trübner & Co., 1901.

"Catholic Prayers: Novena for the Intercession of St. Faustina." http://www.scborromeo.org/prayers/faustinanovena.pdf

Chesnutt, C, W. "Hot-Foot Hannibal." *Atlantic Monthly* 83 (1899), 49-56.

Chesnutt, C. W. *The Conjure Woman*. Houghton, Mifflin & Co., 1899.

Chireau, Y. *Black Magic: Religion and the African American Conjuring Tradition.* Berkeley: University of California Press, 2006.

Collins, D. *Magic in the Ancient Greek World.* Oxford, UK: Oxford, 2008.

Crowley, A. *Magick, Book 4.*

Davisson, Z. "What Are the Teratu Bozu?" 2011. http://hyakumonogatari.com/category/magical-dolls/

Faraone, C.A. "The Agonistic Context of Early Greek Binding Spells." In *Magika Hiera*, edited by Faraone and Obbink, 3-32. Oxford, UK: Oxford, 1991.

Faraone, C.A. *Talismans and Trojan Horses: Guardian Statues in Ancient Greek Myth and Ritual.* Oxford, UK: Oxford, 1992.

Faraone, C.A. *Ancient Greek Love Magic.* Cambridge, MA: Harvard University Press, 1999.

Faraone, Christopher A. "Binding and Burying the Forces of Evil: The Defensive Use of 'Voodoo Dolls' in Ancient Greece." *Classical Antiquity* 10, no. 2 (1991): 165-205.

Frazer, J. G. *The Golden Bough: A Study in Magic and Religion.* 1922.

Haskins, J. *Voodoo & Hoodoo.* London: Scarborough House, 1990.

Hirschfelder, A. B., and Y. Beamer. *Native Americans Today: Resources and Activities for Educators, Grades 4-8.* Engelwood, CO: Libraries Unlimited, 2000.

Holy Bible, 21st Century King James Version®, 1994. Deuel Enterprises, Inc., Gary, SD.

Hudson, W. W. and G. M. Adam, eds. *Modern Culture, Vol. 13.* Modern Culture Magazine, 1901.

Ingemark, C. and D. Ingemark. *Sagor och svartkonst under antiken.* Lund, 2004.

Kotansky, R. "Incantations and Prayers for Salvation on Inscribed Greek Amulets." In *Magika Hiera*, edited by Faraone and Obbink, 107-37. Oxford, UK: Oxford, 1991.

LaCroix, B. *Doll Magic.* Finbarr International, 2008.

Leland, Charles Godfrey. *Aradia, or the Gospel of the Witches.*

Lenormant, F. *Chaldean Magic: Its Origin and Development.*

MacGregor, S.L., trans. *The Book of the Sacred Magic of Abramelin the Mage.* 1897. Reprinted by Dover Publications, 1975.

Meiggs, R. and D. Lewis. *A Selection of Greek Historical Inscriptions.* Oxford, UK: Oxford, 1969.

Miyata, N. "Weather Watching and Emperorship." *Current Anthropology 28*:4 (1987), 13-18.

Negri, S. "Kachina Carving Artistry in Wood." *Arizona Highways* 5 (1993), 15-17.

Ogden, Daniel. *Magic, Witchcraft, and Ghosts in the Greek and Roman Worlds: A Sourcebook.* Oxford, UK: Oxford, 2002.

Olcott, F. J. *Wonder Tales from Baltic Wizards.* Longman's Green and Co., 1928.

Opsopaus, John. *Guide to the Pythagorean Tarot.* St. Paul, MN: Llewellyn, 2001.

Puckett, N. N. *Folk Beliefs of the Southern Negro.* 1926.

Puckle, B. S. *Funeral Customs.* London: T. Werner Laurie, Ltd., 1926.

Randolph, V. *Ozark Superstitions.* London: Oxford University Press, 1947.

Riley, A. C. "Archaeology, Magic, and Engendered Control." 2007. http://www.crossingthethreshold.org/welcome_files/Microsoft%20Word%20%20Archaeology,%20Magic,%20and%20Engendered%20Control%20of%20Domesic%20Boundaries.pdf

Strubbe, J. H. M. "Cursed Be He That Moves My Bones." In *The Practice of Magical Evocation: Instructions for Invoking Spirit Beings from the Spheres Surrounding Us.* Merkur Publishing, 1956.

Tomlin, Roger. *Tabellae Sulis: Roman Inscribed Tablets of Tin and Lead from the Sacred Spring at Bath, Oxford.* 1988.

Winkler, John J. "The Constraints of Eros." In *Magika Hiera*, edited by Faraone and Obbink, 214-43. Oxford, UK: Oxford, 1991.

Wright, B. *Kachinas.* Flagstaff, AZ: Northland Press, 1977.

About the Author

Denise Alvarado was born and raised in the Voodoo and hoodoo-rich culture of New Orleans. She has studied mysticism and practiced Creole Voodoo and indigenous healing traditions for over three decades. She is an independent researcher, artist, spiritual adviser, and cultural consultant. She is the author of the *The Voodoo Hoodoo Spellbook* and is the and Editor in Chief of *Hoodoo and Conjure*, the first magazine journal devoted to the spiritual, cultural and folk magic traditions of the American South. She currently lives in Arizona. You can visit her online at: *www.creolemoon.com* and *www.crossroadsuniversity.com*.

TO OUR READERS